瓊瑤●著

# 我的故事

# 第一部

## 緣起

## 全集自序

## 後記

# Escape from Heng Yang:

## *The Memoir of a Six-Year-Old Refugee Girl*

*Translated by Eugene Lo Wei and written by Chung Yao*

**DORRANCE PUBLISHING CO., INC.**
**PITTSBURGH, PENNSYLVANIA 15222**

The contents of this work, including, but not limited to, the accuracy of events, people, and places depicted; opinions expressed; permission to use previously published materials included; and any advice given or actions advocated are solely the responsibility of the author, who assumes all liability for said work and indemnifies the publisher against any claims stemming from publication of the work.

*All Rights Reserved*
Copyright © 2008 by Eugene Lo Wei
No part of this book may be reproduced or transmitted in any form or by any means, electronic or mechanical, including photocopy, recording, or by any information storage and retrieval system without permission in writing from the publisher.

ISBN: 978-0-8059-7732-5

Printed in the United States of America

*First Printing*

For more information or to order additional books, please contact:
Dorrance Publishing Co., Inc.
701 Smithfield Street
Third Floor
Pittsburgh, Pennsylvania 15222
U.S.A.
1-800-788-7654
*www.dorrancebookstore.com*

## Dedication

*I would like to dedicate this story to my dear friend, Iris Chang (Chang Shun-Ru).*

"Once again, Eugene Wei has managed to teach something to this white-haired educator. In "Escape from Heng Yang," which retells the story of a little girl and her family as they fled from the Japanese invasion of China prior to the end of World War II, Eugene has done a masterful translation of those turbulent days in Chung Yao's life.

This should not surprise me, however, given Eugene's passion for illustrating this important period of history. While I worked on resolutions, first in the California Assembly and then in the U.S. Congress, calling on Japan to apologize for its kidnapping of tens of thousands of women as sex servants to the Japanese army, Eugene toiled through records and eyewitness accounts to find new perspectives into this turbulent time, which he and his family witnessed first hand.

One of Eugene's quests has been to find the Asian counterpart to the "Diary of Anne Frank;" a story that would paint not only the horror, but also the moments of tenderness that sprinkle even the direst human experiences. Eugene knew that among the millions of victims of that occupation, such a story had to exist.

He found it in Chung Yao's story. Eugene went beyond simple translation, however. He built-in the historical context around the original story for non-Chinese readers and in the process, Eugene uncovered yet another dimension of those years. It describes the family's flight through the Chinese countryside and the events the family resorted to, such as acting in a play to raise funds to continue the journey.

*Surely Eugene's work will not allow us to forget, and will help us learn from humanity's inhumanities. That is the only way to ensure a better future. I am personally indebted to Eugene for always teaching me something new as he does in this book."*

–U.S. Rep. Michael Honda
Washington, D.C. Dec. 2007

# Table of Contents

| | | |
|---|---|---|
| Preface | | ................................................. ix |
| Introduction | | ................................................. xiii |
| Chapter 1 | My Flag, My Precious Little Silk Flag! | ....... 1 |
| Chapter 2 | Mama, Don't Go ! | ...................... 6 |
| Chapter 3 | Terror in the Woodshed | ................. 12 |
| Chapter 4 | We Are Chinese (Zhong Guo Ren) | ........ 18 |
| Chapter 5 | Xiao Juan-My "Dry Sister" | .............. 27 |
| Chapter 6 | Captain Tseng and the Chinese Cavalry | ..... 34 |
| Chapter 7 | Riding on a Giant Horse | ................ 41 |
| Chapter 8 | Da Feng Ow-The Great Windy Mountain | ... 46 |
| Chapter 9 | QiLing, XiaoDi, Where Are You ? | ........ 50 |
| Chapter 10 | Drowning In The River | ................. 56 |
| Chapter 11 | The Old Magistrate | .................... 59 |
| Chapter 12 | Ride The Refugee Train To GuiLin | ....... 66 |
| Chapter 13 | My First Marathon ... Oh, My Brothers! | ... 70 |
| Chapter 14 | Goodbye, Captain Tseng! | ............... 74 |
| Chapter 15 | Malaria? Oh, Mother ! | .................. 77 |
| Chapter 16 | Twenty Days In RongHe River | ........... 82 |
| Chapter 17 | Father Sells Yams | ..................... 88 |
| Chapter 18 | I Danced for the Firewood | ............... 93 |
| Chapter 19 | Yams Are Served! | ..................... 99 |
| Chapter 20 | We Won! We Won! The War Is Over! | .... 102 |

# Preface

I was introduced to *The Diary of Anne Frank* when I was a teenager in Taiwan about fifty years ago. In those days I was just beginning to learn English so my ability to comprehend it was rather limited. But I did get the gist of what had taken place in Europe during WWII. In the meantime, both my high school history teacher and my homeroom teacher of Chinese literature gave me some background in the long war of defense against the Japanese invasion and occupation of China from 1931 to 1945. Articles in the newspapers often referred to the horrible experiences of my older generation. But because of the forgiving nature of the Chinese people as a whole and the overt announcement by then president Chiang Kai-Shek to release one million five hundred thousand Japanese soldiers at the end of the war unharmed (the last Japanese soldier went on board a ship from Shanghai some time in 1948 ), the voice of those who had suffered or witnessed the horrible atrocities in the Asian Holocaust were quite subdued. Most of the victims and witnesses just did not want to talk about it. Surviving women from rapes, including those who were forced into sex slavery as "comfort women,"[1], were treated badly by people in their own villages after

---

[1] In January 2001, Mr. Yin represented our APTSJW from Cupertino, CA, and traveled to Hainan Island in China to hand deliver some money to eleven known surviving "comfort women" who were forced to be sex slaves of the Japanese army in WWII. Two of them had died when he got there. But when the local news media publicized it upon the pompous ceremony by local government officials who for fifty-six years had paid no attention to the welfare of the victims, these few women became celebrities. A couple of weeks later, fifty-five other surviving women victims in Hainan came forward.

they went back as if it had been their own fault somehow. Thus, they felt shameful talking about it. Since my parents escaped from Nanjing just before the Nanjing Massacre[2] took place, I did hear a few stories about it as I grew up.

Later on, as I became an adult living and working in the US, I gradually became interested in reading stories about WWII. In a similar manner, as my young hero and my friend Iris Chang who wrote *The Rape of Nanking*, however, I discovered that most of the books written in English were about the European war and the European holocaust suffered by Jewish people and other minorities. When I visited the National Holocaust Museum in Washington, D.C. several years prior to the writing and publication of Iris' book, I learned more about the story of Anne Frank. So as I joined my colleagues at Alliance for Preserving the Truth of Sino-Japanese War (APTSJW) in 1993, I wondered to myself about the possibility of finding a Chinese story during WWII that was similar to *The Diary of Anne Frank*. Iris Chang came to our annual memorial event in December, 1994, when it turned out to be a very meaningful event. Not only was it the first encounter by Iris looking at those photographs on the Rape of Nanjing, which began our friendship and the assistance and cooperation by APTSJW in support of Iris for her work, but it also marked the first biannual conference of Global Alliance for Preserving the history of WWII in Asia (GA).

During WWII, more than ninety percent of Chinese were peasants who were mostly illiterate so that only a very small number of women were able to read and write. My own mother did graduate from Ginling Women's University in Nanjing in 1933, but that was a less than 0.001% lucky minority in China in those days. Both my father's milk mother and my grandmother had bound feet (three inches long) and were illiterate. My mother did keep a diary during WWII, but it wasn't exciting enough. Then in spring of 2003, I

---

[2]The correct perspective of the Nanjing Massacre, including rapes, arson, looting and wanton killing of civilians, should start in November 1937, when one million Japanese reinforcements ( The entire 10th army plus others) in the second takeover battle of Shanghai (first was in 1932) landed in Hang Zhou Bay to break the stalemate between the Japanese China Expeditionary Army and the fierce Chinese defense in Shanghai City since August 1937. Please read: *The Nanjing Massacre* by Honda Katsuichi (English translation, 1999, Pomona College).

discovered the Chinese version of *Escape from Heng Yang* lying buried among all the love stories published by Chung Yao. I shared this knowledge with Iris Chang in 2003-2004 and was encouraged by her to finish the translation into English.

Although Iris Chang has passed on before us, I am sure that she would have been happy to know that I finally completed the translation of Chung Yao's story and am ready to have it published.

Little did anyone know in the years of 1949-1957, while I lived two doors down from Chung Yao, that she was going to become a famous writer some day. I was two years younger than she, so my playmate was her younger brother (XiaoDi in the Escape story) for nearly eight years. They were great neighbors. In those days, however, no one ever mentioned their family exodus experience.

I would like to thank Chung Yao and her husband Mr. Ping HsingTao for their permission to translate and publish her escape story in English. I thank all my friends and relatives for their continued support and encouragement. Friends at RNRC, APTSJW, GA, and Truth Council, here it is to you all!

                            Eugene L. Wei
May 17, 2006, in Washington, D.C. (Book EXPO 2006)

# Introduction

Our story takes place in the spring of 1944. It starts with the family of a young Chinese couple, Chen ChiPing and his wife Yuan XingShu, grandpa Chen and their three children, six-year-old twins and a four-year-old, XiaoDi (little brother). It was the thirteenth year* of Japanese invasion of China counting from 1931. The Chen family tried to escape from the fiery bombed ruins of HengYang in the heart of China, about seven years after the Marco Polo Bridge battles in North China when the young couple first escaped from Beiping (Beijing) to ChengDu in Sichuan. They joined Grandpa in '42. By this time in 1944, there are about one million Japanese troops occupying most of the cities in eastern half of China, including ports and railroads. Heng Yang was the largest southern city in Hunan province, a major railway switching center with a branch

---

*Although Japan had already taken the islands of Taiwan plus LiaoDong Peninsula by force 1895 (the first Sino-Japanese War of 1894-95), the WWII invasion by the imperial army of Japan was started on September 18, 1931, when the Kwantung army invaded ShenYang (Mukden) in Liaoning province of Northeast China (Manchuria). This unprovoked attack was not a sudden move since, among other things, the Japanese troops had moved a huge cannon to ShenYang from Lvshun at the Southern tip of LiaoDong Peninsula many days earlier using the Southern Manchurian Railway. Due to lack of a strong army while trying to take care of its internal problems of war lords and the communists, the government of the Republic of China (ROC) headed by Commander in Chief Chiang Kai-Shek chose the path of no resistance in Northeast China. This action allowed Japan to easily take over the entire Northeast China in just three months. The easy victory prompted Japan to over-estimate its military might as well as to form an insatiable appetite for more territories in the ensuing years. Totally ignoring the intercession by the League of Nations, Japan stalled the talks while staging another attack on China in January of 1932 when Japan used her army air corps on the city of Shanghai for the first time.

of the great Yangtze River separating two halves of the city (similar to Portland, OR).

When General Joseph Stillwell refused to send air drops of food, ammunition, and supplies into Heng Yang City as was requested by General Claire Chennault (12th US Air Force), the poorly equipped Chinese Army was crushed by the invading Japanese forces (in air and on land) after forty-seven days and nights of brave resistance (similar to the Alamo). Our story is based upon Volume # 41 of Ms. Chung Yao's (pen name) books in Chinese : "My Own Story" Part I , from 1944 to 1945.

# Chapter 1.
## *My Flag, My Precious Little Silk Flag!*

Children's memories are sometimes strange in the eyes of adults–only events which seem so insignificant the Chinese termed them "mung beans and sesame seeds." But in my memory, the first item that was related to the war of invasion by Japan in China was a little silk embroidered flag.

One day when I was not even six, I went with my parents to the school where they taught to observe a small track-and-field meet. The first things which caught my eyes were many small flags hanging near the platform where the dignitaries sat and observed the events on the track and in the sandbox area. These were award flags (I later came to understand the meaning) to be given to the champion of each event. They fluttered in the breeze while reflecting the bright sun rays into various colorful tones. I was mesmerized by those flags and asked my mother if I could have just one.

She told me "NO!"

When I insisted, my father looked down at me and said sternly "*Bie HuNao*!" (Don't you disturb the peace!).

I quieted down and just kept sobbing until one of my father's co-workers noticed my condition and came over to offer his consolation (I don't remember his name any more. But he was most definitely a good "uncle").

He took down one of those flags and said to me " If you do a little dance, I will give this flag to you."

In my childhood I was very, very shy. For me to display a dance in front of strangers was "harder than getting up to the sky" as the saying goes. But that shiny little silk flag with its bright and beautiful colors had so much attraction for me I slowly stepped to the vacant spot near the big platform. Those people around me suddenly quieted down while I awkwardly glanced at them and fixed my eyes on my mother for a brief moment.

She smiled at me and nodded her head as if to say "You can do it."

With her encouragement I finally gathered enough strength and started. I did the only dance I could remember at the time, " *Di-Di Pi Juan Liao*" (My baby brother is very tired). I don't even remember if those people applauded, but that dance earned me the small silk flag!

For many days or even weeks, I was completely immersed in my little world of ecstasy with my little silk embroidered flag. I slept with it next to my pillow. I clutched it with me all day, even bringing it to the dinner table. But then the war of invasion and the Japanese soldiers got closer and closer to Heng Yang.

One day the school was forced to close and we were asked to move out of the teacher's quarters. We moved from place to place until we ended up in my grandpa's little house. But that did not last long at all. One night, I was awakened by some heavy cannon shots and explosion of bombs dropped by Japanese bombers into the city of Heng Yang. I crawled out of bed and saw through my half-opened eyelids the fiery scene in the window framed by two men, my father and my grandpa. I shall never forget that scene, because the entire city of Heng Yang was engulfed in flames. Later I learned that the people of Heng Yang fought bravely for forty-seven days and nights. It was similar to the American story of the Alamo, except there were too many Alamos in China.

The next day it was chaos in the village. Mother was busy putting valuable items in big leather trunks and large willow baskets with lids to be lifted by workers employed by Grandpa up to the hay loft in the barn. Mother said that the hay loft was the safest place in the village for our belongings, because the barn contained only some chickens, ducks, pigs, and some bags of rice crop and

## *The Memoir of a Six-Year-Old Refugee Girl*

beans. As I watched her carefully wrapping each item such as scrolls of paintings, fine china, and fine garments and silk dresses and placing them in the baskets or trunks, I thought about my precious little flag. Suddenly, I was afraid that the flag might get stolen by the Japanese soldiers. So I carefully handed it to mother and made sure she placed it among her own treasures in one of the leather trunks. I felt very secure since there was a strong lock on the trunk. I then watched Mr. Huang ( Huang CaiYu was Grandpa's foreman) carrying those trunks and baskets up to the hay loft. That night I slept very soundly because of all that excitement from the previous day. But Mother shook me in the middle of the night, and I woke up to find Father trying to help QiLing, my twin brother, and XiaoDi, my baby brother, get dressed.

Everyone in the farm house was running back and forth. I was in a daze as I heard the sound of gun shots. I walked to the window and looked out.

*Tian Ah*! (My God!) I exclaimed. There was fire all around the village, I heard the sound of people yelling, chasing, dogs barking, chickens and ducks screaming amidst the gun shots and I was scared stiff.

My parents and my grandpa all told us kids to hush up.

Father said in a hurry, "We need to go hide in the hills. Don't make any noise."

I could not understand why we had to hide in the hills. But I sensed that we were in great danger as we snuck out the back door into total darkness. Father carried XiaoDi with one arm while helping Grandpa with the other. Mother just hung onto QiLing and me and pulled us literally forward while we struggled and stumbled through some wild grass and thorny bushes. Our little legs were cut all over, but we didn't dare to cry or utter a sound. Finally we arrived in the middle of a narrow gulch full of huge rocks. We huddled in a tight embrace, hiding among some rocks. The whole night we saw flames shooting up into the sky from the direction of the village. Even the sky was red. Slowly the dawn broke and the sound of the gun shots went farther and farther away. Everything became very quiet for some time.

# Escape from Heng Yang:

    Then we heard Mr. Huang calling us, looking for us. Mr. Huang was happy to find us safe and sound. But then with a sad face, he told us a band of Japanese soldiers attacked our village in the middle of the night, apparently looking for any Chinese soldiers who might have escaped from the city of Heng Yang and hid in our village. No, they did not rob our belongings in the hay loft. They chose the easy way by setting fires and just burned the entire village to the ground. They burned the hay loft with the barn and all our treasured belongings in those trunks. They burned my precious little silk flag! Along with my silk flag went my happy childhood memories. In my recollection this marked the beginning of a whole series of bitter hardship ahead.

# Chapter 2.
## *Mama, Don't Go !*

Huang CaiYu, the forever faithful foreman of my grandpa, helped us find the dried up bed of a small stream with a narrow opening, which led to the winding foot path going downhill to the burned-out village. He brought us an old canvas for the six of us to sit under the stars at night. He then used his hatchet to cut many branches from pine trees and oak trees nearby and blocked the entrance to this gully in the hills. Every day, he risked his own life to walk for miles searching for food to feed us. Along with the food, he would bring us what news he was able to get in the surrounding areas of the suburban Heng Yang city now occupied by Japanese soldiers following a great slaughter.

The reason he made sure we stayed hidden was that while the Japanese soldiers raped young women and girls wherever they went and killed many farmers and pilfered and burned houses and villages at will, they were especially cruel to scholars and teachers like my grandpa and my parents. We had already heard stories about school masters in North China being stripped naked and forced to lay on a wooden bench in January next to the well and have icy water poured on them until they froze to death. We also had heard about the schools in ShanXi Province where the Japanese soldiers would force three hundred (up to six hundred in at least one school) students and teachers to dig four-feet deep holes for themselves, bound their hands behind their backs and then planted them upside-down in those holes to bury them alive. Since my parents taught patriotic themes to their students, they would certainly have been tortured to death if they were caught.

## *The Memoir of a Six-Year-Old Refugee Girl*

For three days and nights the six of us would sit on that small canvas, waiting for Mr. Huang with the news and what little food he could bring to us. I was too young to fully understand what they talked about in hushed tones. But from the haggard faces of my grandpa and my parents, I could tell that the news was only getting worse by the day. Their brows only knitted tighter by the hour. To this day, I still don't know how we were able to pass the time in those three days. I can only remember how my twin brother cried incessantly because he was always hungry. Mother tried to comfort QiLing by emptying her purse of all her treasure, such as the key chain, hair pins, lipstick cover, small comb, small mirror, just to keep him quiet and to direct him to things other than food. But even after pocketing a whole bunch of noise-making toys, QiLing was still crying for more food. Three and half year-old XiaoDi was so young that he was totally unreasonable. When he was awake he would look up in the trees for bird nests or crawl into the tall grass looking for locusts. His only merit was he fell asleep a lot. When he had nothing to do and nothing to eat, he would also cry. But soon he would cry himself to sleep. Of the three children I was the most quiet. Most of the time I just sat there in a trance, thinking about my little silk flag and all the lost moments of happiness. I was oblivious to what was around me half of the time.

On the first day, Mr. Huang brought two full bowls of rice for the six of us to divide. On the second day, the two bowls were no longer full, but we licked them clean to the bottom. On the third day, Mr. Huang did not appear in the early morning as before. I heard Father telling Grandpa that he was worried about Mr. Huang's safety. We were all very hungry as QiLing and XiaoDi started crying again. Somehow the sun seemed to slowly move from one side of the gully to the other side. Under the pressure of no food and no water, even I broke my silence. QiLing cried for food while XiaoDi cried for water. I also started to sob and tears streamed down my face, because my stomach was growling in pain. The three of us started a chorus that really annoyed my father. He sternly ordered us to keep quiet and hush up. Grandpa just shook his head and sighed. Mother clutched XiaoDi with her left

## Escape from Heng Yang:

arm while encircling me with her right arm trying continuously to comfort us. That little gully was filled with our noise.

But just at that very moment we heard a clear gun shot from the foot path nearby. We saw the shadow of a man swiftly passing outside our barricade made of tree branches. We all were scared into total silence. We forgot to cry or holler and were speechless. I peeked out from the crevices of that barricade and saw a Chinese farmer stumbling forward with one leg dripping wet with blood. He was still running even with one injured leg! Then I heard the shouting of some Japanese soldiers and some more gun shots. I saw the farmer fall down and saw him die. Tears of fear came streaming down my cheeks as I saw blood gush out of his lifeless body that was alive only a moment before. It was the first time in my life witnessing and suddenly understanding how death could come to a person. My body trembled in total silence.

While XiaoDi went burying his head into my father's long gown and shook like a leaf, Mother tightly clutched QiLing with her left arm and covered his mouth with her right hand to keep him from crying out loud. Her face had turned snow white. Grandpa's lips moved noiselessly cursing the brutal act by the Japanese soldiers. Time stood still as if for a century.

Then we heard the soldiers' footsteps walking away one by one. By some miracle they did not discover us in hiding. Long after seeing those soldiers disappearing down the hill, Mother let out with a huge sigh while her face turned from pale white to a shade of green. QiLing struggled quietly from her clutch and sat there taking deep breaths. He forgot altogether about his hunger.

XiaoDi slowly moved out of Father's lap, with his bright, big eyes rotating he stuttered, "Gun…gun...what …what...a… very, …very, … long…gun!"

Mother extended her arms to embrace XiaoDi as he continued his stutter " But … guns…guns…there are…are…some guns!"

As Mother followed her gaze from XiaoDi upward, she suddenly froze in midair with her arms still extended toward him. We

## *The Memoir of a Six-Year-Old Refugee Girl*

all looked up and saw a row of Japanese soldiers standing on top of the hill pointing their long rifles down at us, without making a sound. My two younger brothers and I slowly squeezed into the outstretched arms of our mother. For several seconds we just looked at them while those soldiers just looked at us without a sound. Then a Japanese officer wearing spectacles jumped down into our gully and pointed his pistol at Grandpa.

The Japanese officer spoke and gave his order in Chinese. " Stand up. Let me search."
Reluctantly, Grandpa stood up and let him search his pockets.
The officer found money, calling cards, fountain pen, and school emblem, pocketed the money and holding all the rest in one hand and said, "A teacher, huh?"
Grandpa kept his silence and bit his lips. Likewise, that officer searched Father's pockets and cleaned up all his cash.

Fortunately, Mother had hidden her purse in the tall grass a few hours before. She stood and patted her thin cotton dress showing no place to hide any money. But the officer was still pointing his gun at Grandpa while looking at his school emblem and his calling cards, apparently trying to decide what to do next. The air in that gully was frozen and I could see Mother's lips turning white.
Suddenly, my twin brother QiLing discovered a surge of courage and walked straight forward to face that Japanese officer. He said, " You don't need to search me. I will give you everything I have." So he took out everything from both of his pockets: mother's key chain, lipstick cover, small comb, hair pins, the small mirror, along with his marbles and a few pebbles. He offered all that he owned and handed them to the officer.
The officer was startled by QiLing for a short moment. Then a smile went across the corner of his mouth as every soldier on the hill top busted out with laughter. Amidst the laughter, the bespectacled officer discarded Grandpa's other belongings and jumped out of the gully. He waved at his soldiers as if commanding them to go. Apparently, the lives of my grandpa and my father were spared. But a tall, stout Japanese soldier with an ugly, coarse face jumped out

# Escape from Heng Yang:

from behind the line of soldiers with guns. He carried a huge stick as he jumped into the gully roaring something in Japanese. His shirt was unbuttoned with his hairy chest half-exposed.

That soldier grabbed Mother by her wrist and said in broken Chinese, "You, follow me !" As he made his command, he started to drag Mother toward the top of the gully. My usually civilized and gentlemanly Father just exploded and ran up to Mother, holding her with both arms while shouted at that big soldier, "Let her go, you beast! Let her go!"

Everything happened so fast. The soldier swept his big stick on my father's waist and knocked him rolling down the slope into the bottom of the gully. Then Grandpa also could not stand by watching it and rushed toward Mother and the soldier. With a second powerful sweep with his stick, he also knocked my grandpa down the gully. He continued to drag my Mother up the slope as Mother sat herself down, trying to grab at the long grass with both of her hands, kicking, crying, and screaming.  The mixed feelings of anger, fear, and a sense of helplessness fell on me like a ton of bricks, as I grabbed hold of the corners of Mother's cotton dress and belted the loudest cry with every ounce of my lungs. My two brothers also ran over and each hung onto one of mother's legs and cried out loud.

We screamed,:"Mama, don't go! Mama, don't go!"

As we cried, Mother also cried. The big soldier loudly cursed in Japanese. He dragged even harder as we sensed a losing battle. Mother's body was beginning to slip away from our little hands.

Then out of the blue, the bespectacled officer appeared to have a bit of mercy in his heart and shouted something in Japanese to the big soldier. The soldier loosened his grip on my mother's wrist, which had turned black and blue by this time. The two of them exchanged a few harsh words. Then the officer pointed at the three of us children crying in the heap piling on top of our mother, and spoke to the soldier for quite a long while with a very solemn face. Finally the big soldier turned and jumped out of the gully with reluctance and carried his big stick with him as he walked away.

## *The Memoir of a Six-Year-Old Refugee Girl*

The three of us crawled into Mother's arms and continued our crying. When we all calmed down a little, we discovered the Japanese officer was still standing there, watching us as if in a daze. He waited for us to stop crying a bit and jumped back into the gully. He gently grabbed XiaoDi and pulled him toward his side, wiped away his tears with a handkerchief and turned toward mother.

"How old is he?" he asked.

With trembling voice mother replied, "Almost four."

That officer looked up at the clouds in the sky and said thoughtfully, "My son is about the same age as he." When this was done, he jumped out of the gully, waved at his soldiers and walked away without turning back again.

We remained in shock for a long time after they were gone. None of us could believe that we were able to just slip by a major calamity so easily. It was many, many years later when I realized that even among those seemingly heartless Japanese officers and soldiers who tortured and killed millions of our countrymen and raped countless women, some of them also had families with wives and children, some of them still had a shred of human mercy left in them. Perhaps that bespectacled officer was even a college graduate from somewhere.

Father and Grandpa crawled up the slope from the bottom of the gully by this time. The six of us just looked at one another for a while, as if we had been separated from one another for a life time. Our parents tightly clasped their hands together. Father tried to examine Mother's dark blue wrist. The shock had not entirely gone away. The three of us hung onto them sobbing, not sure if we ought to let go of them just yet.

Grandpa picked up his walking stick, stabbed at the ground and said, "You cannot stay here in Hunan anymore. I am too old to tag along with you. But you two are still young. Take these young ones and get out of this area fast! Try to get back to Sichuan if you can. Go! You must all leave as soon as possible."

Father stared at Grandpa for a long time. They both knew separation was inevitable. But neither of them was quite ready to face that reality yet.

# Chapter 3.
## *Terror in the Woodshed*

It might have been several days or even a week after we left the gully before the woodshed incident. But it was not our first choice, as you will see when I continue my story. All I can remember is that we had to run from farm house to farm house, from village to village and had to hide from the Japanese soldiers as well as the Chinese spies who had been bought by the enemy invaders. Sometimes we stayed in one place overnight. But more often we could only stay for an hour or two before moving on. We were like the birds forever scared of the sight of a bow after barely escaping from a fast arrow (*Jing Gong Zhi Niao*). We were also like the few fish that had just snuck through a broken hole in the bottom of a fishing net (*Lou Wang Zhi Yu*). I remember seeing and hearing village after village getting its share of pilferage, fire, and people being killed or women being raped by the marauding Japanese soldiers. Stories of teachers or students being tortured and killed in large numbers made us hide ourselves even more cautiously.

Before the woodshed incident, however, we somehow met up with one of my father's younger cousins and his family. In my memory uncle Biao-Shu was married to a very petite but beautiful lady, Biao-Shen. They brought their one-year-old baby boy with them. My little cousin was a very chubby and cute baby boy. Biao-Shen let me hold him a few times and I played with him and cuddled him to sleep.

Soon after the two families merged, we moved to a cluster of

## *The Memoir of a Six-Year-Old Refugee Girl*

farm houses deeply hidden in a bamboo forest. The farm houses belonged to an old farmer who used to work for my grandfather in his youth. Over the years, he earned enough wages to purchase his own land and built his own home. Behind their houses was a path leading to a mountain so in times of need, one could easily run into the mountain and further hide from danger. This old farmer and his wife were a typical couple of hard-working, honest and kind people in the old Chinese countryside. They welcomed us with open arms.

But out of my grandfather's and my father's expectation, that farm house cluster was already full of people taking refuge from outside of the bamboo forest. Many other local scholars and well-to-do business people and even village chiefs from miles around had already gathered here, because it was the only good hiding place in the tri-county area. What none of us could have expected, however, was that this "secret" hideout was already discovered by the Japanese soldiers!

The old farmer told my grandfather: "There were three batches of Japanese soldiers looking to catch 'suspicious' people just yesterday. I had one of my nephews watching the road outside the bamboo forest. As soon as he saw any *GuiZi* he would run in here to warn us. This way they all ran into the hills in a few minutes and they were not found."

*GuiZi* was used by all Chinese people to describe the invading Japanese soldiers. Literally it meant something like "short goblins". He was beaming with pride as he said it.

His wife was a very kind and sweet woman. They not only made sure we received their full-scale hospitality, but also told us how to hide, how to take the shortcuts into the mountains, etc. It was by this time that we learned how many people they had already saved in just a few days in the bamboo forest. They treated everyone the same way!

It was in the early afternoon when we arrived in the bamboo forest, tired and hungry after another long and fearful series of run-and-hide with very little in our stomachs. My head was already

## Escape from Heng Yang:

reeling with fainting spells from hunger. So we all sat down to eat as soon as they brought us into their kitchen area where a table full of food was waiting for us. Soon after we picked up our chopsticks, however, we heard people running and yelling in the farmyard.
But before we could ascertain what was happening, the farmer's wife rushed in while waving her hands in desperation and yelled, " Hurry! *GuiZi* are here! You must run for the mountain. Hurry! Hurry! Hurry!"

Father and Mother quickly threw down their chopsticks and came to help us off the benches in the kitchen. My twin brother, Qiling, just sat glued to the bench, refusing to leave the table and the bountiful food. XiaoDi had a mouthful of scrambled eggs and struggled to stay. Biao-Shu and Biao-Shen simultaneously jumped to the bed where the baby had just fallen asleep to pick him up.

Amidst all this confusion and chaos came the old farmer. "There is no time now, everybody! There is no time for you to run to the mountain. GuiZi came too fast this time! You must find a place to hide right here! " He surveyed the rest of his farm house. The nine of us were dumbfounded as we looked around for a place to hide in his scarcely furnished farm house where there were no huge furniture or closets to hide in.
Then his daughter-in-law rushed in and said, " *GuiZi* are already in our farmyard. Other people have all gone to the mountain. Only the Chen family is still here."

The old farmer's wife instantly made her decision and dragged both my twin brother and me while motioning the rest of us to follow her. She moved quickly and quietly with us in tow, through the back door of her kitchen and rushed around the chicken coop. She opened the door of the woodshed and pushed all nine of us inside. She quietly warned us as she retreated and closed the door from the outside,: "*QianWan BuYao Chu Sheng!*" ( Tens of thousand times no sound out of here!)
All nine of us just squeezed tightly together in that small woodshed. We all looked at one another very quietly. We even minimized

## *The Memoir of a Six-Year-Old Refugee Girl*

our breathing sounds. Terror had seized us all in that moment.

I still remember QiLing holding his chopsticks in one hand and mumbling
very quietly, " *Wo Eh Le. Wo Yao Chi Fan.*" (I am hungry. I want to eat rice.).

Mother tried to cover up QiLing's mouth while father attempted to look for a switch to bolt the door of the woodshed. But there was no switch! Farmers had no use for locks and switches to bolt their woodsheds.

There were some large crevices on the door of the woodshed. We could see half of the farm yard. I was sure the Japanese soldiers could see us inside the woodshed if they even half-tried. This was probably the worst place in the world for a bunch of women and children to hide. I remember hanging onto my mother's dress while she encircled XiaoDi with one arm and held QiLing's mouth with the other hand. I was quietly shaking with fear. My legs were like mud.

While we all stood there with our backs butting against the piles of firewood, we could hear the sound of the boots worn by the Japanese soldiers coming closer from the front of the farm yard as they searched the seven or eight houses built by the old farmer, one by one. We heard the yelling of commands in Japanese by their officer. We heard the banging shut of doors, the voice of the old farmer trying to explain something to the officer, farm furniture being thrown about, some boxes of belongings being tossed around, and the cursing words by those soldiers when they could not find any suspicious people in hiding and could not find anything valuable. Then we heard the noise made by chickens and ducks as they were caught and their throats were cut.

Then the searching team went past the chicken coop and headed toward the woodshed. We could hear the loud protest by the farmer's wife about losing her dog and her pigs a few days ago and now losing more chickens. Mother tightly held XiaoDi and covered QiLing's mouth to keep him from uttering a sound. But no one expected my baby cousin to suddenly wake up from Biao-Shen's soft arms and started to cry. Biao-Shen quickly opened the top of her dress to feed him. But the baby refused to suckle and just cried. Biao-Shen tried to cover his mouth with her hand, but she could not completely muffle his crying sound. His face turned bright red as he tried to struggle free from Biao-Shen's hand.

Grandpa sighed and said quietly, " Our fate led us to this woodshed. What was coming must now come!"

Biao-Shu's face turned white as a sheet as he took a sad look at everyone of us in the woodshed. His look appeared to have very deep meaning. (It was many years later when I finally understood the meaning of that look of terror). Then he quickly took the baby out of the lap of Biao-Shen and covered his mouth with one hand and tightly squeezed the baby's neck with the other arm as he sat halfway on a wood pile. I saw the baby's face turn blue as he stopped making a sound. I froze in total terror, because that was my baby cousin being tightly squeezed. Biao-Shen jumped over to him trying to get the baby back.

She cried as she screamed at him, " What are you trying to do? Kill him?"

Biao-Shu replied, " Yes, I must strangle him so we don't have to all die because of him!"

Biao-Shen screamed as tears came streaming down her face, "You are crazy! Why don't you strangle me first!" She tried to pry Biao-Shu's arm loose with all her might.

Biao-Shu said, "We must do what is right. We cannot let a little baby's cry get two families killed, especially getting our cousin's family killed." He held tight.

Just at this moment, we heard the opening and shutting of the door at the chicken coop and the noise of many chickens being let loose and scattered all around, screaming as they ran toward the front of the farm yard.

Then we heard the Japanese soldiers chasing after those chickens. One of the soldiers in the search team, however, did not follow the chickens. He used half-clear Chinese and ordered, "Open the door!" He meant the door of the woodshed.

## *The Memoir of a Six-Year-Old Refugee Girl*

Then we heard the old woman, " *Lao Tian Ye*! (Oh, my God in the sky!) Why would you want to inspect the outhouse?" She added, "Even the door has no bolt, how can anyone hide in there?" Years later I thought that although she had never gone to any schools, she still deserved the best actress award in Hollywood. So that soldier turned and went around to the front yard. As the sound of that Japanese soldier's boots moved farther away, Biao-Shu let go of the baby, and Biao-Shen quickly grabbed him and turned her back to Biao-Shu. Then I saw the color in the baby's face returning to normal as he let out a weak cry that was gently muffled by Biao-Shen.

We all sighed a great sigh of relief as the farmyard slowly returned to peace and quiet. Then the old farmer's wife opened the door to the wood shed and said, "What is going on in here? With all your baby's crying and you people yelling, I had to let loose another cage full of chickens and shoo them flying all over the yard just to cover up your noise."

We all looked at one another with disbelief. Another miracle! We had just escaped from another kiss of death fate! I was only six, not yet able to fully appreciate it at the time. But when I saw Biao-Shu hugging Biao-Shen and the baby and kissing them like a crazy man, I was able to sense the preciousness in their love for one another. How complicated his feeling of love for his baby and his sense of duty to stifle his sound to preserve the lives of others in the woodshed. In that moment, I must have grown up another ten years. This type of experience in me must have contributed to my early maturity in later years.

# Chapter 4.
## *We Are Chinese (Zhong Guo Ren)*

In the next few days, not knowing why, we were again separated from Biao-Shu, and Biao-Shen, and their baby boy, my little cousin. My father now realized that the farm cluster in the bamboo forest was no longer a good hiding place. As a matter of fact, there was not one inch of land in the entire county of Heng Yang that was safe any more. All I can remember is my parents sometimes stayed up all night discussing two pressing issues. One of them was how to safely cross the lines of Japanese soldiers unnoticed. The second issue took them the most time. It was whether to take Grandpa with us in our attempt to escape from Heng Yang on the long journey to ChongQing. At that time my grandpa was close to eighty years of age, definitely not suited to the long journey. But my father just could not feel safe to allow Grandpa to stay in the occupied (by Japanese) zone.

They finally came to a decision on the separation issue. Grandpa was to be escorted back to his old home where he was born in the less traveled township of Zha Jiang, which was several days walking distance from Heng Yang county. I still remember how we all worked on changes of clothes and used make up to pretend we were farmers. But regardless of how my father tried to disguise himself by wearing the rough and short two-piece garment of a farmer and used dirt to color his face, arms and legs, his near-sighted eyeglasses were a dead giveaway. My mother's pure Beiping (Beijing) accent, plus her delicate movement and gesture, were hard to cover up. But we were determined to escort my grand-

## *The Memoir of a Six-Year-Old Refugee Girl*

pa back to his old home. So we said goodbye to the kind old farm couple, left the bamboo forest, and headed toward Zha Jiang.

This one day was a day of curse! It was a stormy day, without wind and waves, and a day full of drama. It was a day I will never forget. About two hours after we started walking on a small country dirt road, we encountered the first Japanese road block.

"Stand still and be inspected," roared the leader of the pack in Chinese. So the six of us all stood still. The officer leading those soldiers walked authoritatively toward us, sizing my grandpa and my father up and down. My parents both kept quiet in order not to expose their identity as teachers. The officer ordered two of the soldiers to search Grandpa first. I could see how angry Grandpa was, because I seemed to detect fire coming out of his eyes and the blue veins bulging on the side of his temples. But he stayed still as they moved their hands up and down him, searching for weapons. They took what few bills were left in his pocket and cleaned him out. Then it was my father's turn.

This group of soldiers did not make it more difficult for us. After they took money carried by my father, they just let us go. Without making a noise, I guess they did think that my mother, now looking old and ugly, was some old farm woman with a dirty kerchief over her head. So we all walked forward quietly. None of us kids dared to speak or make any noise. At that time in our childish minds, those soldiers were but a gang of robbers. It was much later when I realized the shame and humiliation that must have befallen upon my parents and my grandpa.

Then we came upon a second band of Japanese soldiers around noon.

"Stand still and be inspected," was the same familiar roar in Chinese by the officer. This time the soldiers found no money on my grandpa and my father, but they found a sheet of paper with Chinese written on it, folded and tucked away in my grandpa's inside pocket. The officer could not read it so he just crumpled it and threw it on the ground. They cursed in Japanese and walked off in a huff.

# Escape from Heng Yang:

Father took a long breath and sighed his relief. He asked Grandpa, "Dad, why don't you just throw away that darn poem?"

"No," replied Grandpa, as he picked up that sheet of crumpled paper with his shaking hand, carefully smoothed it out, folded it and put it right back into his inside pocket.

Later, Mother told me it was a long poem written by Grandpa describing the atrocities committed by the Japanese soldiers for thirteen years in China since September 18, 1931, when they first attacked ShenYang in Northeast China.

Some of those verses had described the massacre at Ping Ding Shan (Flat Top Mountain) when more than two thousand men, women, and children from eight or more villages and towns were gathered by Japanese soldiers on a large grain-drying field under the mountain top for "picture taking," which had turned out to be machine guns all around them covered with black cloths. Then the top of that mountain was blown off with preset explosives over the victims, many of whom were buried alive. Other highlights in Grandpa's poem had included the defense of the Marco Polo Bridge outside of Beiping (Beijing) by brave Chinese soldiers who fought over the iron railroad bridge and took it back three times from the attacking Japanese troops in July 1937, and the fierce battles of defense by Chinese peasants and soldiers over the city of Shanghai in the summer of 1937 when three hundred thousand Japanese soldiers with overwhelming fire power tried to take over the city for the second time but succeeded.

Many verses in that poem were used to describe the huge onetime rape and slaughter of three hundred thousand Chinese civilians in Nanjing (Nanking) in December 1937. Had the Japanese officer been able to read Chinese, we would have all been killed that day for sure. I was too young to have comprehended that poem at the time. But years later my father taught history at the Normal University in Taipei (Taiwan) during my high school days and I finally learned all the details.

After some rest under a tree, we started again on our way. Before long we were stopped by a third pack of Japanese soldiers.

"Stand still and be inspected," came the familiar roar from their officer in charge. But Father had gone through enough searches by this time. He simply pulled every pocket lining inside out to show the Japanese officer there was no more money on him. Although that officer did not understand the mumbling by my father, he saw the pocket linings hanging from my father's pants and noticed the family of tired and haggard-looking woman and children. So he let us go after some moments of sizing us up and down.

Even as young as I was, after encountering three bands of Japanese soldiers who had behaved like robbers in one day, I was able to sense the danger we were in; the entire country side was crawling with Japanese soldiers.

Fortunately, all three groups of Japanese soldiers were merely interested in our money and were not searching for pretty women. Had they wiped off or washed the dirt off Mother's face, it would have been tragic. Or if they had suspected Father of being a teacher, he would have been tortured and killed. By sundown, we were all very tired, hungry, and thirsty. Encounters with other groups of enemy soldiers could happen around the bend in every road we took. XiaoDi began to complain and cry about the pain in his legs. So Father picked him up and carried him piggyback. Soon we discovered we were on a stretch of deserted dirt road without any signs of life around. When we came upon a fork in the road, Father stopped and put XiaoDi down under a large tree. He discussed with Mother and Grandpa and tried to decide which road we ought to take. They had lost their directions.

Then as if he were an angel from heaven, a farmer appeared from one of the roads carrying with him two stacked bamboo baskets on his back and a bamboo stick in his right hand. Those baskets were usually used for carrying farm produce, so my parents thought perhaps he had sold his produce at the market and was on his way home. Both Grandpa and Father got real excited. What could be more exciting than meeting another Chinese person after being stopped by three groups of Japanese soldiers all day and getting lost in the deserted countryside?

## Escape from Heng Yang:

So Grandpa went in front of that farmer and smiled as he asked him, "Did you encounter any GuiZi (Japanese soldiers) on your way here?"

The man looked straight at Grandpa as if not comprehending what he had said.

So my father, feeling that maybe Grandpa did not make it clear enough, supplemented by saying, "What is on that road ahead where you have just come from? Did you come across any Japanese soldiers? We are trying to avoid them."

The man moved his gaze from Grandpa to Father without cracking a smile, contrary to the behavior of most of the farmers in Hunan Province. Slowly he took those bamboo baskets off his shoulders and laid them on the ground in front of him. His gaze was still fixed on my father. At that point father must have felt something not quite right.

He tugged at Grandpa's sleeve and said, "Let's go, Dad. Let's not ask him for directions."

But that man quickly stopped Father and said in excellent Beijing Chinese accent, "Don't you go! Stand still and be inspected!". At that command, my parents were both dumbfounded and the face of Grandpa turned white as a sheet. By that time, the three of us children had become accustomed to those words of command so we just stood frozen. In an instant we all understood what was going on and who he really was. He was a well-educated Chinese spy who, like my father, had put on farmer's clothing and even carried props like those bamboo baskets as a disguise. In order to conquer China for more land and more resources, those Japanese soldiers fought in the name of their emperor. This Chinese spy, however, was much more dangerous and terrifying than his employers because he looked and spoke like a Chinese native. He was a traitor!

That man now pointed his finger at Grandpa and said, "Stand still! I want to inspect you first." They always wanted to inspect him first. But this time Grandpa looked at him straight in the eyes and exploded, "No! I will not be inspected by a Chinese traitor!"

## *The Memoir of a Six-Year-Old Refugee Girl*

I saw the man's face turning iron green. He quickly opened the lid on the basket on top and whipped out a pistol. "All right, then," he said as he raised that pistol at Grandpa. " Listening to you talk, I can tell what kind of person you really are. You are not a farmer. Are you hiding something on you so you won't let me search you?"

At this juncture, Grandpa's face turned very ugly. My parents exchanged a quick look at each other. The air was heavily laden with tension and fear. I thought about that folded sheet of paper with the long poem hidden in Grandpa's inside pocket. I knew that my parents and my grandpa were worried about the same thing. This Chinese traitor could read it and could easily betray us.

"Don't you even touch me!" Grandpa spoke with determination and with authority.
He continued, " I have already been searched by three groups of Japanese soldiers today. I will not be searched by a Chinese traitor!"
With that the farmer-looking man became very angry. He roared at my grandpa, "All right, if you don't want to be searched, then I will gun you down!" He waved his pistol as if to show he was serious.

Grandpa stood even straighter, with his white hair fluttering in the wind; it was a glimpse of him I could never forget. He said, "Even if you should gun me down, I would never let you search me."
At that, the man cocked the pistol and started to take aim at Grandpa.
Father ran up with his back toward the gun and pleaded with Grandpa, "Dad, please let him search you, please!"
Grandpa stood firm, pushed Father aside with an unusually strong shove and said, "*Bu Xing* (Not allowed)! I would rather die right here than to be searched by him." Turning toward that man again, he said, " Why don't you just kill me and let my son and his family go?"

The man seemed to be softened a little. He replied, "You are a stubborn old man, huh?" He appeared to be bewildered, paused for a moment and said, " I only want to search you. I don't want to kill you. Do you value the search more than your own life?"

Grandpa answered him with true grit, " Yes, you can gun me down. But I won't let you touch me as long as I am still alive."
The man raised his pistol again. It appeared that Grandpa's life was hanging on a shoe string. Even XiaoDi, the three-year-old, could sense it. He started to cry in fear.
Father knelt in front of Grandpa while tears came streaming down his cheeks and begged, "Dad, please let him search you. Please! Please!"

Grandpa spoke with a soft voice, but everyone could clearly hear him, "Search or no search, I am going to die soon anyway. Son, you can let him search you. Then you can all go peacefully to ChongQing after I am gone."
Then Mother also knelt down beside Father. She said to Grandpa, " All right, Dad, if you are going to die, let us all die together, the whole family."

XiaoDi was always the most precious grandchild of Grandpa. He now understood that the "bad" guy was going to kill Grandpa. So he ran to Grandpa, hugged his one leg and screamed, *"Ye Ye Bu Yao Si ! Ye Ye Bu Yao Si* (Grandpa, don't die!)" QiLing, my twin younger brother and I could not endure it any longer, either. We both ran over, crying and hugging our parents. I quickly grabbed the other leg of my grandpa. In a unison chorus we all screamed, " Ye Ye Bu Yao Si!"

Grandpa bent down and embraced us three grandchildren with both of his arms. But he remained adamant as he said, "No search, no search, no search !"
The man appeared befuddled by our family drama. He stared at all of us for what appeared to be an eternity and said nothing. Then, lowering his pistol, he roared brusquely at us, "Sop crying ! Why don't you all just go?"

## *The Memoir of a Six-Year-Old Refugee Girl*

Father stood up incredulously and asked, "Go ? Don't you want to search us anymore?"

The man looked straight at my father and replied plainly, "The search is done and over with. You can all go now." He opened the lid of the basket and threw his pistol in it.

Still unable to believe the new verdict, Father asked him again, " You mean the whole family?"

"Yes, the entire family." The man sighed deeply. Then he lowered his head and with his bamboo stick now in his right hand, he wrote the following three words in the dirt: *Zhong Guo Ren* (We are Chinese). He pointed to himself and then to us. Then he moved a couple of feet to one side and wrote three more words: *Ri Ben Ren* (They are Japanese). Upon writing the second three words he pointed in the north-western direction, indicating where the Japanese soldiers must have been located at that time. After that he said very softly, "Why don't you all go east."

As soon as he said this, he quickly erased all those words in the dirt with his sandal, picked up and shouldered his bamboo baskets, and walked toward the north-western direction without turning back again. For quite some time we all just quietly stood there, trying to regain our senses. Without saying a word, we slowly started to walk toward the East. That night we found a flat spot in the woods on a hillside and huddled together for the night, being thankful that Grandpa was still with us and was still alive. In the morning, we found the main road to Zha Jiang and kept going. By nightfall, we finally safely arrived at Grandpa's Orchid Garden home in the township. All day long we did not encounter another single Japanese soldier.

Many, many years later I can still remember those three words in the dirt, *Zhong Guo Ren* (We are Chinese). For a very long time I was puzzled by that man's change of behavior. Was he good or bad, I wondered. As a traitor, why then did he let us go free and tell us which direction to go? Thus, the concept of who I was and which country I belonged to was not taught by a teacher in the classroom of a school. I had to think hard on it and had learned it under the barrel of a gun. I had to grow up much faster in the middle of a war of aggression by a foreign power.

# Chapter 5.
## *Xiao Juan – My "Dry Sister" ?*

It was semi-restful at my grandpa's Orchid Garden house in Zha Jiang township, because we did not need to play hide-and-seek with Japanese soldiers for a while.

Zha Jiang was not a military hot spot by measure of both sides and was located within the Japanese "occupied" territory. Thus we were spared of searches for a while. But then came the night to start our journey to ChongQing.

My parents talked with Grandpa until late in the night after our travel luggage was ready. The three of us grandchildren took turns to hug and kiss Grandpa goodbye. We all left the Orchid Garden house around midnight. I remember that it was the night of a "left-over" moon (at end of a lunar cycle) with speckles of a few stars in the sky. People on the farms went to bed early so there was not a sound around, neither chickens nor ducks, not even the barking of a dog. It was so quiet a night—anxiety of the unknown lurched in the dark. I was not afraid. But I could sense the danger lying ahead for us in the journey.

In the front yard there were two *tiao fu* waiting for us (*tiao fu* is an experienced laborer who carries balanced loads on his shoulder with a strong bamboo stick). Each of them had a strong bamboo stick and two large, weaved bamboo baskets. XiaoDi would sit in one of those baskets to balance the one with our farmers' change of clothing, plus other needed items such as water and dry food. QiLing and I each sat in one basket to balance each other out over

# Escape from Heng Yang:

the shoulder of the second *tiao fu*. This was going to be a very long journey by foot, heading south through the provinces of GuangXi and GuiZhou before we could arrive in Sichuan to ChongQing. At that time in 1944, the direct route upstream the Yangtze River through the Three Gorges was already blocked by heavy battles between China and Japan so all refugees had to take the long way around.

Ever since my birth, I had already been on many vehicles of transportation including the sedan chair, mule cart, charcoal-burning trucks and buses, trains, boats and even a hand-pushed "Rooster Cart" riding on a single large wheel up front with an iron axel supporting the frame which allows two long poles extending backward for the pusher of the cart. It was very similar to a wheel barrow, except the cargo or the passengers were distributed on the frame at both sides of the wheel. The ride would save on the feet and legs, but not on the behind. But sitting in a bamboo basket and being carried by a *tiao fu* was a new adventure for me.

Curiosity for the basket ride did dilute my feeling of sadness in my departure from Grandpa. But when I saw tears welling in my parents' eyes as they held Grandpa's hands in silence, I was blanketed with the taste of "life or death" separation, which kept me speechless for a long time. I just sat quietly in the front basket, listening to the "thump, thump" of the *tiao fu's* heavy footsteps in the dirt plus his rhythmic breathing with a heavy load on his shoulder. QiLing also kept his silence while sitting in the rear basket. We did not talk to each other all night.

We were told to travel by night and rest by day. This night we were supposed to cross over the most stringent fire line of the Japanese soldiers. If we were discovered by the Japanese sentry at fixed points or by their circulating inspection teams on the road, it would have meant certain death to all of us, including the two *tiao fu*. Our parents had warned us several times before the trip began to keep silent and refrain from coughing out loud. We were actually shocked into silence by all the events we had gone through by this time that we knew our lives and deaths were separated by a very

## *The Memoir of a Six-Year-Old Refugee Girl*

thin line. Our total silence was virtually guaranteed as the three of us were soon rocked into sleep in those bamboo baskets.

We all wore black or dark clothes, including the two *tiao fu*, and we carried neither lanterns, nor torches, nor any storm glass lamps sometimes used by farmers. The route we chose consisted of all winding, country dirt roads to avoid the Japanese sentry points. The two *tiao fu* seemed to know the country roads in that region like the backs of their hands. It was most likely not their first attempt to guide people across the enemy lines.

This time, however, they were hired (and paid dearly) by Grandpa to carry and escort us all the way south into GuangXi Province. Father was to pay them the second half of their wage after we arrived in one of the train stations in Northern GuangXi. We were told that once we safely crossed the provincial line into GuangXi, we could get on the refugee train, which would carry us to GuiLin. From GuiLin, there would be frequent trains going through GuiZhou Province all the way to Sichuan and to ChongQing. Later I learned all this was a one-sided wishful thinking by Grandpa and my parents since the entire trip took one-and-a-half years until Japan surrendered. By then, I had already celebrated my seventh birthday on the run.

One time, I opened my eyes to the sloshing noise of the *tiao fu* walking in water and in mud. Father tried to guide them through a rice field by separating the rice stalks in front of them. I sat up in the basket and watched them moving ever so slowly across the rice field until we all safely arrived on a new dirt road. Both *tiao fu* rested us and the baskets in the dry dirt while they wiped off the mud on their feet with a bunch of long grass and again put on their straw sandals. Mother went over to a ditch to wash off the mud on her lily-white feet and sat down to put her socks and shoes back on. I noticed the blisters on both my parents' feet. But they never complained. After some rest, the *tiao fu* balanced the two baskets on each bamboo stick and started their "thump, thump" and rhythmic breathing down the road again. We continued our journey in the darkness.

# Escape from Heng Yang:

When I think about it today, I now know that my parents had no guarantee of safety across the enemy lines at that time. The only thing which sustained them to move on was their raw courage and their determination.

Those "night run" days were not too long. In the daytime, we were allowed to stay in farm houses (mostly mud walls covered by roofs made of straw). At night, we continued our trip. Traveling while sitting with our legs folded in the bamboo baskets was not very comfortable at all. After a while, our legs became numb and sore. So we frequently asked to be let out of the basket to walk around. It turned out to be a welcomed request because both *tiao fu* could use frequent stops to give their tired bodies a rest. But since our legs were short and we were really too young to endure a long march, we could only walk for a little while before asking to go back into those baskets again. Although we were quite lucky in not meeting a single Japanese soldier during these nights, we did come across a fair number of towns and villages that had been pilfered and/or molested by the Japanese soldiers. Some villages had been burned to a crisp, just like the one where our belongings, including my little flag, was torched by them several weeks before. But the most unforgettable encounter for me was a little girl named Xiao Juan.

In my memory, the details leading up to finding Xiao Juan are not clear because none of us had anticipated the encounter. It seemed as if we had heard her crying from a distance and we just followed her sound until we found her lying on the dry spot of a rice field. My parents joined hands, carrying her to a grassy area under a tree and gave her something to eat. Her clothes were all torn ragged and she had cuts and bruises all over her body. Her face had not been washed for quite some time. In an exchange of questions and answers, we knew both of her parents had been killed in a village that was robbed and burned by a bunch of marauding Japanese soldiers. She was extremely lucky to have survived the holocaust. She cried as she told us what had happened to her family and her village. The mud and dirt and dried-up blood on her body

# *The Memoir of a Six-Year-Old Refugee Girl*

struck a chord in my heart.

I was always an emotional child when I was growing up. I asked Mother, "Mom, can we take her with us, please?"

That girl, with her large black eyes, looked at Mother with such an imploring, anticipating, and helpless gaze it stayed in my memory even until this day. Mother sighed deeply, took the girl into her arms without saying a word. She wiped the girl's face clean and gave her more food. In my mind and my heart, Xiao Juan was to be a permanent member of our family and she was to stay with us forever. In those days of war-torn China, families picking up stray children was a very common practice.

Thus, using the easy excuse of my sore butt and my numb legs after sitting for too long, I let Xiao Juan sit in my bamboo basket, while I walked right by the basket as it moved forward. I suddenly found a great deal of strength in my walk. I murmured to Xiao Juan everything only "dry-sisters" would share with each other. Yes, I accepted her as my "dry-sister" through the rest of that night's journey, just short of a ceremony. A "dry-sister" is a Chinese way of recognizing the close relationship between two girls who are not related by blood.

In the morning, we arrived at a farm house whose owner allowed us to rest for the day for a small fee. Mother gave Xiao Juan a tub bath and put ointment over her bruises and cuts. Then she put on my clothes and shared the same bed with me. We held hands and fell asleep murmuring to each other on the same pillow. Before I fell totally asleep, however, I seemed to have overheard my parents discussing the next phase of the trip. It seemed we were going to finally cross over the last Japanese sentry point that night. Then they changed their subject to Xiao Juan. They talked about human nature, economics, and terms I could not understand. Then their voices slowly diminished to a murmur as I drifted into a deep sleep. I was simply exhausted from the excitement in meeting Xiao Juan and the long walk in the night.

As day light turned to evening and into another dark night, I

## Escape from Heng Yang:

was gently awakened by Mother's shaking of my shoulders. As soon as my eyes were opened, she placed a finger on my lips trying to signal silence to me. As I sat up Mother warned me not to wake up Xiao Juan. Still half-asleep, I dressed quickly and was led out of the farm house. It was a moonless night as a thin veil of clouds shielded us from starlight as well. After the *tiao fu* carried us for a little while, the cold breeze finally woke me and I struggled to stand up in the basket while holding to its sides. I shouted, "But Mother, you guys have forgotten Xiao Juan!"

Mother held me down in the basket and said to me apologetically, "*Feng Huang,* dear, we are barely able to take care of ourselves for the long trip. We really just cannot take on another little child." She continued, " Besides, Xiao Juan has an uncle in another village not far from that farm house we just left. That farmer knows her uncle very well. He promised to take her to her uncle today and we have left him some money for Xiao Juan. That is the best we could do for her and you should be able to understand by now."

"But Mother, you had promised to take Xiao Juan along with us. You promised…." I protested feebly as I sat back down in the basket, tears welling out of my eyes.

Mother sighed deeply without saying another word. Father also came over to give me his order to stop my complaining. His words and his solemn face spelled the end of the conversation. So I did not dare to make any more protests. The bamboo baskets moved silently forward as the thump, thump of the *tiao fu* walked with the load on his shoulder and his heavy breathing rhythmically accompanied us through more rice fields and across a small bridge over a creek.

I shrank into a ball in the basket and just wept uncontrollably. The feelings of a child are very strange. I did not cry when we were parting from my beloved grandpa. But when we left that farm house with Xiao Juan in it, I just could not help myself. This time I cried for a very long time, because I kept thinking what she would do when she would wake later, finding us gone. I kept thinking how disappointed and heartbroken she'd be. Many years later, I finally understood that my parents really had no choice at the time,

## *The Memoir of a Six-Year-Old Refugee Girl*

because it was already a very difficult task for them to take the three of us on that long journey to Sichuan.

# Chapter 6.
## *Captain Tseng and the Chinese Cavalry*

Captain Tseng, how can I ever forget Captain Tseng! The biggest miracle since I was born was our encounter with this man during our one and half year of escape journey out of Heng Yang. I dare say had we not met him, our entire family history would have to be rewritten. But what kind of a person was this Captain Tseng?

As we finally crossed the last Japanese line of sentries in southern Hunan, all we saw was bright and warm sunshine over a wide roadway and teams after teams of Chinese army with horses and heavy equipment moving south. We no longer needed to play hide-and-seek with the Japanese soldiers. We were not afraid of being caught or being killed anymore. We were overjoyed to be able to travel free from fear! The family of five with the three of us riding in the bamboo baskets carried by the two *tiao fu* simply followed the railroad heading south to GuangXi. But after we continued this way for a few days, we discovered the circumstances around us were not as simple as we had anticipated.

First of all, we discovered there were not many refugees like us traveling south on the same road. Those who had wished to escape from Heng Yang had gone way ahead of us, because either they had no young children like us or they did not dilly dally or have to escort their older generation backward to their hometowns like we did. Any farm hands or owners of small farms who remained were heavily bound to their farms. Secondly, we happened to have been caught right in the middle of the historically famous "Xiang-Gui"

## *The Memoir of a Six-Year-Old Refugee Girl*

(Xiang = Hunan, Gui = GuangXi) withdrawal of all Chinese armies after the defeat in Heng Yang region in 1944. Thirdly, we were often pushed aside by the on-rush of heavy equipment trucks and by the Chinese cavalry. Well-coordinated formation of Chinese foot soldiers as well as wounded soldiers on carts and trucks also gave push to the unwanted civilians like us. Other times we actually caught up with the slower-moving heavy equipment trucks or stalled vehicles and wounded soldiers so we had to halt for them before moving on again.

Mother had never suffered such hardship in her whole life. Despite the fact that my maternal grandparents had been educated people who did not believe in bound feet for my mother, she still came from a relatively well-to-do family where a *Qian Jin Xiao Jie* (young lady worthy of a thousand ounces of gold) never had to toil or do hard labor or walk on a country dirt road heading to nowhere fast. But she seldom complained. I noticed the huge blisters on her feet. When those blisters broke, I saw blood trickling down from her shoes into the dirt below as she limped onward. The two *tiao fu* were also getting tired and weary of the long trip. Although they had been paid half of the wages by Grandpa with the second half to be paid by Father after our arrival in GuangXi, they began to complain of a much longer journey than they had bargained for because of all the extra zigzag roads we had to take to avoid the Japanese sentries. Father just kept persuading them to stay with us through the course and he raised their pay to keep them from taking off without us.

All of us were getting very exhausted at this point and our progress was getting slower by the day. Then, the Japanese bombers started to fly over us. Oftentimes, those noisy bombers would get louder as they approached us and would roar as they shrieked past overhead. ( **Note**: The Chinese Air Force was still in its infancy during WWII. For eight years of defensive war from 1937 to 1945, less than fifteen hundred Chinese aviators died in fighting simply because they had neither enough trained men nor enough airplanes. American fliers who died fighting the Japanese over China numbered over three thousand. That's why the Chinese military and civilian casualty was so high in that defensive war. Japanese engineers forced Chinese laborers to extract large amount of bauxite in conquered territories of North China and shipped the bauxite back to Nagasaki to make aluminum in order to build more fighter planes and more bombers for the war.)

Although the Chinese army was in retreat, the soldiers moved in very orderly formations. All foot soldiers wore bundles of straw or leaves over their shoulders so that they could simply roll over on the side of the road in a camouflage from the air. The horses and the heavy equipment would try to find trees or large rocks to hide themselves under. But the Japanese bombers seldom threw any bombs over the retreating Chinese army. Their mission, it would appear in those days, was to bomb the cities and towns, which were still occupied by the Chinese defending forces. Occasionally, however, these bombers would fly low and would spray their machine gun bullets at the Chinese on the ground. That was totally terrifying to us who were defenseless and often had no place to hide.

One day near noontime, we heard the faint engine noise of Japanese bombers from the horizon. Again, all the soldiers near us rolled over into the ditches on the side of the road as the horses and heavy equipment and cannons were led under some trees. Our family found a large tree to hide under. On the other side of the tree were a few uniformed Chinese officers with their horses. They appeared to be the Chinese Cavalry escorting the heavy equipment and supply trucks driven by soldiers. One of the officers was holding the reins of his horse as he looked at us with some degree of curiosity. I paid very little attention to the officer. I was immediately attracted to his big brown horse. The horse stomped his feet in the dirt as he breathed heavily through his nostrils. I had never been so close to a big horse like this before. With one hand on my basket, I just stood there mesmerized by such a handsome animal.

My father, after watching the Japanese bombers disappear and looking at the soldiers hiding at the roadside and our haggard family bunch under the tree, made a statement as if to himself, "How

## *The Memoir of a Six-Year-Old Refugee Girl*

much must we continue to pay for the greed of and persecution by a foreign nation?" Wearing farmer's clothing while speaking like an intellectual, my father gave himself away quickly.

That tall officer with the big brown horse tied his horse on a lower branch and came over to us. He asked Father, "You are not a farmer, are you?"

Father, now facing a Chinese officer instead of a Japanese, answered him calmly, "No, but I am a teacher."

Hearing this, the eyes of that officer seemed to light up as he reiterated, "Oh, so you are a school teacher, eh?" He then pointed to Mother and inquired, " Is she your wife, then?"

To that father replied, "Yes, and she is also a teacher."

" I see. But where are you guys traveling to?"

"Sichuan," answered Father.

"Do you realize how far it is to travel on foot all the way to Sichuan?"

" I know," said Father. "I had known how far it was going to take even before we started on this trip. But we must go there because we don't want to stay in the enemy-occupied territory and be treated like second-class citizens."

Listening to that remark, the officer appeared surprised and just fixed his gaze at Father. At that point, I finally moved my eyes from the big horse to look at the officer. He had a square face covered under a cap and a crew cut, with large ears and big eyes under thick eyebrows. He was not only very tall, but also had broad shoulders and a thick chest like his big horse. He gave me the ideal image of a living, breathing, battle-toughened professional Chinese soldier! I became interested in the way he studied Father. Later on, I realized perhaps he had never met a Chinese Don Quixote and a bookworm like my father. He said, " You don't expect to travel like this all the way with these *tiao fu* carrying your children to Sichuan now, do you?"

Father replied decisively, "We plan to get on the refugee train. But if we could not get on the train, we'd walk some, rest up some and walk some more until we get there."

The officer shook his head and said very seriously, " There is no way your family could make it that far by walking."

"But we must keep going even if we should all collapse. We have no other choice."

The officer paused for a moment and said, "I have observed you and your family for a while. You people who have read many books are so strange. Although I have never gone to school, I have a lot of respect for teachers. So let me point out a way for you that might help you at least get to GuangXi."

Father became curious. "What way is that?" he asked.

"As you well know by now, the Chinese army is making a major retreat from Hunan to GuangXi and other locations. The attitude of most of them is very bad. Tempers flare under these terrible conditions. Sooner or later you would get their wrath. What you must look for is a regiment of soldiers and officers from GuangXi Province, because they know this route very well and because they are going back to their own territory. Once you get protection from them all the way into GuangXi, you might have a chance. "

"GuangXi regiment?" Mother had kept her silence up to this point. She said, "But there are so many of you. How can we tell which one of you are from GuangXi?"

The officer pushed back his cap and pointed to the insignia on his upper arm with a broad smile, I am an officer from GuangXi. If you wish, I can protect your family to get there."

My parents were both caught by surprise. They exchanged a deep look at each other in disbelief. Later I realized they had to decide whether this man was good or bad at that moment. But after a brief moment of consideration, Father extended his hand to the officer and said, "My name is Chen, eh … Chen ZhiPing. We sincerely accept your offer to help us and we want to thank you."

## *The Memoir of a Six-Year-Old Refugee Girl*

The officer grabbed Father's soft hand in his big rough hand and replied heartily, "My name is Tseng Biao. "I am a captain in the 27$^{th}$ regiment from GuangXi. I am a cavalry officer in charge of some heavy equipment and supplies for my regiment."

So this was Captain Tseng. From this point on, we became his responsibility. We even ate the army rations carried by his men and drank out of their canteens. Captain Tseng became our guardian angel and changed our fate and our lives forever.

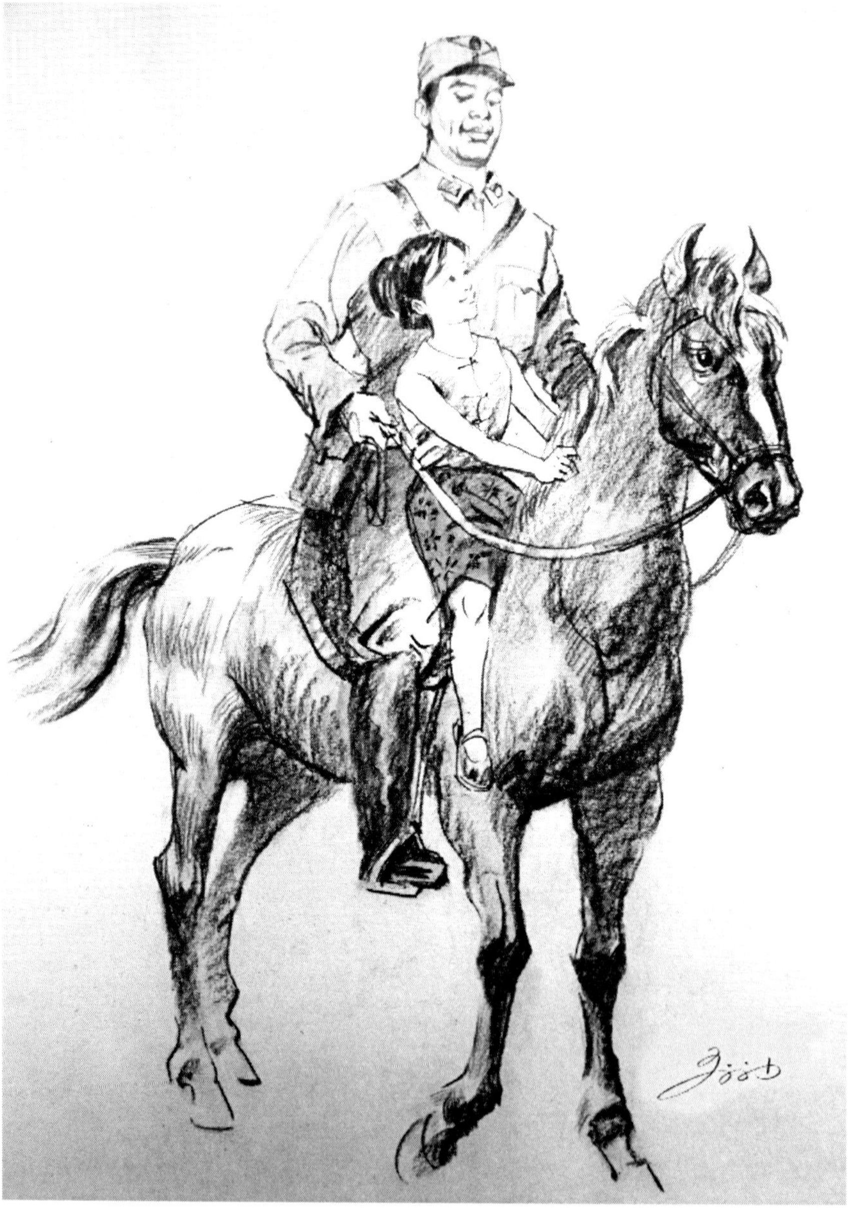

# Chapter 7.
## *Riding on a Giant Horse*

Regarding the memory of those days we traveled with captain Tseng, it was a time I will always remember and treasure, because it was a time full of danger, adventure, a sense of trust and security in his company, but it was my first experience riding on a giant horse!

As soon as we started our trip together with the Chinese cavalry and the supply and equipment convoy, Captain Tseng noticed the severe limping of my mother as she walked. So he gave an order to one of his lieutenants to let Mother ride on his horse. Lieutenant Wang immediately obeyed the order and led his horse over to Mother. It was a big red horse that dwarfed Mother by a huge margin. The big red kept shaking his head and breathed heavily while spewing a lot of hot air over Mother. He also kept stomping his hoofs in the dirt. Mother was scared out of her wits.

She kept saying as she retreated backward, " I will walk. I'd much rather walk on foot!"

"*Bu Xing* (No way)! said the captain in his booming, baritone voice. He knitted his thick eyebrows together as he gave his orders as if Mother had become one of his soldiers, "Just get up on that horse. You must ride on that horse, and there is no second way about it."

Mother did not dare crossing Captain Tseng. So she gingerly approached the horse and, with the help of Lieutenant Wang, tried to climb up into his saddle. But as soon as Mother tried to mount, the horse gave a loud shriek as if he knew Mother was not his mis-

# Escape from Heng Yang:

tress. Mother was so scared, she stumbled off the stirrup and just turned and ran. This caused all the soldiers and officers now watching this comedy to roar in laughter.

Captain Tseng did not laugh. He just moved into Mother's path and stared down at her with a solemn face. Mother stopped and looked up at him. Captain Tseng softened a little and motioned with his head toward the horse as if to say, "Don't be afraid. I am here to make sure that you will not be harmed."

Mother obediently turned and walked back to the horse again. This time, Lieutenant Wang not only held the reins tightly but helped push Mother up on the saddle. But this time the big red just whinnied and raised his two front hoofs while arching his back to throw Mother off. Mother hung onto the reins and screamed with terror.

This time, even the Captain could not help but crack up. He shook his head and motioned for Lieutenant Wang to help Mother off the big red. Then he untied his own brown horse and led him over to Mother and simply commanded, "Change horses!" while the Lieutenant gently let Mother down from his red horse.

As it turned out, Captain Tseng's big brown horse was a very well-trained military horse that had seen real battle conditions and was not easily spooked by any new riders. So when Lieutenant Wang helped Mother into the saddle of the big brown, he just stood silently waiting for the next order. Captain Tseng made sure of Mother's comfort and safety by ordering a soldier to lead his reins. Captain Tseng loved his own horse so much he usually would not let anyone ride him. So with Mother, it was an exception. I noticed that Mother's cheeks had lost their natural color for quite some time after this incident.

Thus, with the *tiao fu* still carrying the four baskets with the three of us in them, we set out again on the road under the Captain's care and his orders. Traveling with the army meant very little stop and go. Now that mother was riding and no longer limping along, we gained more ground even with the convoy of trucks and heavily loaded vehicles. Sometimes we did some night marching with the army. So after another couple of days the *tiao fu* began

## *The Memoir of a Six-Year-Old Refugee Girl*

complaining to Father that they could not take it any longer.

They said, "If we keep on going like this without any stops, we will die of exhaustion. We are no soldiers and we want no part of this kind of fast army march."

Captain Tseng heard the commotion and came over to them. He said, "You two had made your promise to carry these baskets with the children in them all the way to GuangXi. How dare you not to go through with your promise before you get there?"

The two *tiao fu* chose not to talk back and just shrank into the corner under a tree. One of them, however, was still murmuring his complaint to the other.

Captain heard it and slapped his big hand on the butt of his pistol in the holster with a loud noise while walking over to the tree. He said, "Which one of you doesn't want to go with us anymore?"

That made both of them just shut up for good for the rest of the day. So we continued to move forward like an army. We only stopped for supper by sundown. The army cooks had arrived ahead of us and had already started the fires when we arrived at the camp.

After removing the baskets with QiLing and me in them, one of the *tiao fu* removed his shoulder pads to examine his shoulder. The thick callus had broken and he was bleeding from his shoulder. The hurried schedule probably had exceeded his limit. Father saw it and winced. Captain Tseng happened to be standing nearby and saw it, too. But he did not even knit his eyebrows.

Later when the troops were ready to move, however, Captain Tseng led a horse over to Father and said, "Mr. Chen, why don't you ride this horse with your daughter so that we can lighten the load of the *tiao fu* and travel faster?" In the meantime, he ordered each *tiao fu* to carry only one child in the front basket and balance it with clothing and supplies in the rear baskets. The fulcrum, which was the shoulder of each *tiao fu,* was adjusted forward because the rear basket was much lighter. Father happily complied, but not for himself necessarily because he was walking without any load on him.

Captain Tseng held the bridle of the horse to allow Father

mount up the saddle. Then he picked me up and placed me in front of my father. He asked, "Mr. Chen, you do know how to ride a horse, don't you? "

Father replied, "No problem. I am not like my wife …" But before he could finish his sentence, the horse swung her head to the left and then put her two front legs up in the air! In the blink of an eye, both Father and I were thrown off the horse. Father held me in his arms for dear life, so I was not even scratched. I was only stunned by the fall, but Father ended up groaning in pain. I soon started bawling at the top of my lungs, mostly because I was scared. Fortunately, Father was not injured either. Both of us landed in the dirt. Mother quickly ran over to see if I was hurt. She gently picked me up and dusted me off to examine my whole body. When the soldiers saw we were unharmed, they just burst out into a huge laugh.

Father slowly stood up, appearing embarrassed as he mumbled half to himself, "It would appear that this horse does not have any good feeling toward me."

Captain Tseng laughed heartily and said, "Mr. Chen, you might be tops in reading books, but you still need some help in riding a tough horse." Then he looked at me and said invitingly, "Why don't you ride with me then?"

I shook my head like a toy drum on a stick with small hammers on strings as I shrank backward into Mother's arms.

The captain said, "I am an expert on a horse. You see, I will not let you fall off her." He reassured me with some fancy controlled moves and jumped off and on, while the horse made a tight circle. Without waiting for my mother's permission, he scooped me up from Mother's arms when the horse came close by me and my mother. Then he jumped right back into the saddle of the horse. He held me with one arm while holing the reins with the other hand and said, "All right, what do you think? Aren't we riding nice and steady?"

I did not utter a word. In my childhood memory, this Captain Tseng was coarse but brave, handsome and god-like. He was like a knight in shining armor whom any woman would have fallen for, let alone a six-year-old little girl. I was in awe of him, but I felt very secure.

## *The Memoir of a Six-Year-Old Refugee Girl*

Then he put the reins in his left hand which held me and raised his right arm and yelled: "Forward, march!" At his command the entire caravan of horses, wagons, and trucks started to move with the foot soldiers following close behind.

As the horse trotted forward, I felt the breeze on me and I began to enjoy the ride. I looked back at my two brothers still being carried in those bamboo baskets by the *tiao fu*. I knew I got the best deal, while they were bobbing up and down, to-and-fro. My fear of falling off the horse quickly went away as the captain's big hand held my tiny waist. I turned and looked up at Captain Tseng and saw his warm and smiling face.

He said, "I have two sons, and I have always wanted a daughter. I want my daughter to look just like you."

I cracked a smile at him, but I said nothing because I was so very shy!

He continued, "From now on you can just ride with me until we get to GuangXi."

I was so lucky I got out of the bamboo basket for good. XiaoDi grumbled in jealousy while QiLing was madder than heck. Little did we know this new arrangement was going to cause my brothers and I to play strange roles on the trip.

# Chapter 8.
## *Da Feng Ow-The Great Windy*

Soon we came to the *Da Feng Ow* (the Great Windy Mountain') that would lead us to GuangXi Province. Although there were several highways all leading to GuangXi from southern Hunan, we were pressed with little time available, because we were followed by Japanese army in close proximity. Due to Chinese army intelligence information, however, the best route at that time was to cross the Da Feng Ow directly. Captain Tseng studied the map with two of his officers and made a decision to cross the mountain.

There were guides in the army, but none of them had ever been up this mountain because they had spent most of their lives in southern Hunan and most of the highways leading south. Apparently Da Feng Ow had no strategic value. The natives had this saying: "Up seven, down eight and ten around" to describe this mountain. No one really understood the meaning except that it was a very strange mountain. It was full of snakes and other ferocious animals and thorn bushes and weeds. Once Captain Tseng made his decision, however, no one would stand in his way. The captain decided to abandon some of the heaviest equipment they could not carry, divided all the rest of the supplies evenly among his soldiers to carry on their backs and allowed the horses to carry the remaining equipment too big for the men. Only a few wagons were drawn with us. The trucks were led by one of his lieutenants and were driven on the highway around the mountain. They were to meet us up ahead because they could go much faster covering a much longer road. Then he gathered all his horses and the cavalry to lead

## *The Memoir of a Six-Year-Old Refugee Girl*

the way up the mountain. Even Mother had to let go of her horse so it could go up front.

I was still sitting on Captain Tseng's big horse while my brothers remained in those bamboo baskets being carried slowly up the mountain. It was exciting being up front and sitting on the lead horse. But my excitement soon waned as the sharp blades of those long weeds started to slash into my legs. Those weeds had grown taller than a man in the mountain. While the captain and his men wore long pants with tall boots I only had my short skirt on with my legs dangling over the sides of the horse. As the horse moved up the mountain through those weeds, my legs got cut over and over again. Captain Tseng was totally focused on the movement of his troops going up that he did not notice the cuts on my legs. I thought at the time that a good "cavalry girl" should not cry. So I just gritted my teeth and endured it.

Our group had started early in the morning. At the age of six, I had no idea just how far a *Li* was (about one-third of a mile). Seven *Li* up the mountain was merely a local description. But I was sure it had to be at least three times longer than that, because several hours later we were still going straight up! Now the sun was beating down on everyone, with no streams or other sources of water in sight. The only things grown in that part of the mountain were thorns, weeds, and rocks. Most of the soldiers had already emptied their canteens halfway up the mountain. There were no roads and it was getting steeper while the hot sun pursued us in vengeance.

Soon one of the soldiers fainted under his load which caused some commotion. Captain Tseng ordered everyone to stop and rest. There were no trees in sight so we used our shirts or jackets as umbrellas, while Mother took out her umbrella from the bamboo basket.

When the captain lifted me off the horse, he noticed the cuts on my legs and exclaimed, "Oh my! Why didn't you make any sound with so many cuts on you!"

I then started to sob. How could he understand that a good cavalry girl riding next to her god was not supposed to complain? He quickly summoned his medic to put ointment on my legs and gave

## Escape from Heng Yang:

me his canteen. I noticed while others had emptied their canteens, his canteen was almost still full. I sensed the importance of water at the time so that after a couple of small swallows, I gave it back to him. The captain* then handed it to my parents and my two brothers. Each of them only took a couple of mouthfuls. Then he gave the canteen to the soldier who had fainted. By the time it came back to him again there was not a drop left in it.

So we continued upward on our way. The treacherous climb now involved many huge rocks that even the horses were going slower than the men. Although the foot soldiers did not dare to complain, I was able to tell they were getting weaker with every step they took, while each of them carried a heavy load on his back. Captain Tseng got off his horse and led her by the reins with me still sitting in the saddle. At this time, one of the engineer soldiers was stumbling upward at a short distance behind us. Captain Tseng saw him staggering to the point of falling down, so he dropped the reins of his horse. The horse obediently stopped while the captain walked back toward that soldier. He promptly removed the load from the soldier and took a second look at his horse. Apparently he decided that the horse was too tired to take another load. So he simply slung that load over his left shoulder and helped the soldier up the rock with his right arm. The soldier thanked him and started to move forward by himself after a short respite. Some time later in the afternoon, we finally reached the top of the rocky mountain.

We all stood on what appeared to be the highest flat rock and looked down. Everyone was momentarily stunned by the view. Then all the soldiers started to cheer. As it turned out, on the south side of the Da Feng Ow Mountain there were trees, grassy meadows next to many peaks, which seemed to have risen right out of flat ground and a large river running through it all. It was the grand

---

*This "iron man" in Captain Tseng left such an extremely deep impression on me that all the male heroes in my novels written many years later were modeled after him. As an example, one of my books entitled "Six Dreams" had a story under the name, "Song of a Drifter," in which I simply used Captain Tseng for my character model as the hero in that story.

## *The Memoir of a Six-Year-Old Refugee Girl*

view of a beautiful paradise beyond description. Yes, water! The cheers went up from the beleaguered soldiers not because of the beauty in the scenery below but because of all that water in the river. It was GuangXi Province!

So they all went crazy. Every soldier started to rush down the side of the mountain even with his load on his back. There went the military restraint. This was the only time I saw Captain Tseng loosen up on his men and let them go freely downhill for water.

The captain simply smiled as he watched those soldiers slip and slide down some slopes to the point of falling in a heap sometimes. They yelled in happiness as they ran until they all arrived at the shore and unfastened their load as they jumped into the river with total joy. We all started to go down the slopes with the horses and wagons in tow. Somehow I also ended up in the shallow part of the river. My entire family soaked in the cool water and splashed it at one another until we were all dripping wet. Ever since the night we had said goodbye to my grandpa on the escape journey, we were in a sad mood. This was the first time we were able to relax and laugh heartily again as a family. That night we all camped by the river and had a good night's rest. For once the future seemed brighter than we had dared to dream about. We were finally in GuangXi Province.

# Chapter 9.
## *QiLing, XiaoDi, Where Are You ?*

In the morning, the army started to move again from the river. Our target was a large city in northern GuangXi called *Dong An* (Eastern Peace). But now with all the heavy equipment, trucks (they caught up with us in the night), tired horses and foot soldiers, we were slow-going through some winding hilly narrow paths after we left the river camp. By nightfall we merely made it to a small town called *Bai Ya* (white teeth) and Captain Tseng ordered everyone to stop and camp outside of town. It is worth noting that Captain Tseng tried hard not to camp inside any towns or villages to avoid disturbing the residents by keeping his soldiers from temptations.

I remember one night back in Hunan, we camped inside a small town. In the middle of the night, we were awakened by two gun shots. At first, everyone thought the Japanese troops had caught up with us and our soldiers had started to battle with them. Later we learned one of our soldiers was caught stealing a sugar cane. Captain Tseng had confirmed the soldier was definitely in the wrong ( there were witnesses) and executed him on the spot.

My father disagreed with the captain's decision and argued with him saying, "How could the life of a human being be equal to a sugar cane?"

Captain Tseng explained although stealing a sugar cane was a minor matter, the Chinese army must not go through towns acting like a bunch of hungry locusts and make trouble for the civilians. He reminded my father that troubles caused by the Japanese troops in their "burn all, loot all and kill all" policy was bad enough for

## *The Memoir of a Six-Year-Old Refugee Girl*

our people. "Besides, it is the most basic principle of discipline in the Chinese army since three thousand years ago," he asserted.

At the time I felt very strange to hear it for the first time and could not understand what he had done. But I wasn't about to question God.

So we camped just outside of Bai Ya. The army cooks had already started the fire even before we arrived. Soon after we found the tent we were supposed to sleep in, we heard one of the cooks calling us to supper. Mother took me to the area where the cooks had served up a huge pot of rice porridge that smelled heavenly and ladled several bowls for our family. After handing a bowl to me, she began to look for my two brothers.

She called, "QiLing, Xiaodi, come and have supper!" But there was no answer. So she went into the vacant area calling, "QiLing, XiaoDi, where are you?" The pitch in her voice became higher and she sounded a little scared.

At this time father came over and joined her. Their frantic voices sounded loud and shrill in the night air. "QiLing…Xiaodi…Where are you?" After walking through the entire camp, they discovered that the *tiao fu* with those bamboo baskets and my two brothers had all vanished.

Now the entire army unit was stirred up. Captain Tseng came over and accompanied my parents in search of my brothers among his soldiers. By this time in our journey, those two *tiao fu* had been mingling with the soldiers for many days and had earned my parents' trust in them. Mother went up to every soldier and asked him if he had seen the *tiao fu* or my two brothers.

But the answer was the same every time, "No."

No one had seen them since we left camp by that big river.

The soldiers up front thought that they must have fallen behind with the rear group. But those soldiers in the rear thought that they must have gone to the front of the line. The fact was that no one had the leisure to look out for anyone else while he was trying to go forward with the army through very difficult and narrow paths as fast as he could.

# Escape from Heng Yang:

My parents lost their appetite for supper. They blamed mostly themselves for not keeping a closer watch over my brothers.

Captain Tseng tried to calm them down, saying, "Don't lose hope. Our original target was the city of Dong An." He continued, "We only decided to stop here in Bai Ya for the night at the last moment. Maybe they went on ahead and have already arrived in Dong An City." He concluded, saying, "One never knows, maybe they are looking for us this very minute in Dong An somewhere. We will start earlier in the morning tomorrow. I'll bet we will find them just as soon as we get to Dong An."

The captain had a way of reassuring people and calming them down. Since his analysis was not unreasonable, my parents did quiet down some. But they still could not go to sleep. They just sat up waiting for dawn to arrive. That night turned out to be one of the longest in our lives. We kept our eyes open for the rest of the night, although I did doze off in mother's lap a couple of times. Mother quietly mumbled to herself while sobbing that she was so careless. Father tried to comfort her by saying some reassuring things. I just prayed that they must be waiting for us in Dong An. They must!

Finally it was dawn. The army quickly cleaned up after breakfast and started on our way. Before long, we could see the city walls of Dong An on the horizon. But as we walked through the city gate, we were all bewildered by what we saw. For ordinarily, Dong An was a large city with a sizable population of civilians. But the Chinese government had decided not to defend that city, so every civilian was ordered to evacuate from the city. We found all the houses empty with their doors wide open and many other Chinese army units camping all around the city. Dong An was turned into a giant army camp!

The *tiao fu* with the bamboo baskets and my brothers were nowhere in sight. So Captain Tseng ordered several of his soldiers to go through the entire city looking for them. Soon they all came back empty-handed. My parents became extremely disappointed by this time and were distraught. Even the always calm Captain Tseng was visibly shaken. But very quickly he decided to backtrack. He said, "Since we took the hilly path through narrow and winding roads to Bai Ya, maybe the *tiao fu* took a different road and it was much longer than ours. Maybe they stopped for the night somewhere and arrived at Bai Ya after we had left."

So the captain sent two pairs of fast riders back to Bai Ya. Soon the first pair of riders came back empty-handed. They got to Bai Ya through a shorter road, but did not see the *tiao fu* or my brothers. After what seemed a very long time the other two riders also returned. But they came yelling their report to Captain Tseng that they not only did not see my brothers in Bai Ya, but also encountered some Japanese soldiers who shot at them. So they returned fire as they mounted their horses and quickly got out of that area.

Their shouting message was soon spread throughout the city of Dong An like a wild fire. At the time, the Chinese government wanted to preserve the strength of every army unit in order to select a good place to give the Japanese invaders a major setback. They were ordered not to waste their ammunition and their men in any skirmishes. So every unit in Dong An began to withdraw and move on toward their own assigned location. Captain Tseng's group of one hundred fifty men were carrying heavy equipment and supplies and ammunition so they also must leave the city and move further south into GuangXi.

After giving orders to his soldiers and watching them move, Captain Tseng came over with his horse and gently picked me up and jumped into his saddle. He shouted at my father, " Mr. Chen, you are still young yet. How can you worry about not having any sons? Your life is more important now. So let's go!" Perhaps he thought that if he carried me with him, my parents would follow. But my parents just stood there looking straight ahead at nothing in particular.

As the horse was pulling away, I struggled with all my might and slipped from Captain Tseng's arms as I cried out, " Mother!" and rolled down from the horse. I fell feet first in the dirt but landed backward on my butt. Then the horse took off like an arrow as the captain grumbled something to catch up with his soldiers. His duty was most definitely with his army unit and he had already spent too much time searching for my brothers.

I managed to pick myself up and stumbled toward Mother. She came forward and clutched me tightly with her arms. Thus the three of us stood together and watched the army units disappear from the horizon. Dong An became a ghost town. Not a single animal stirred. The wind blew over pieces of paper with the fallen leaves and dust. The three of us just stood there with our minds focused on my two brothers. I quietly repeated to myself, "QiLing, XiaoDi, where are you?"

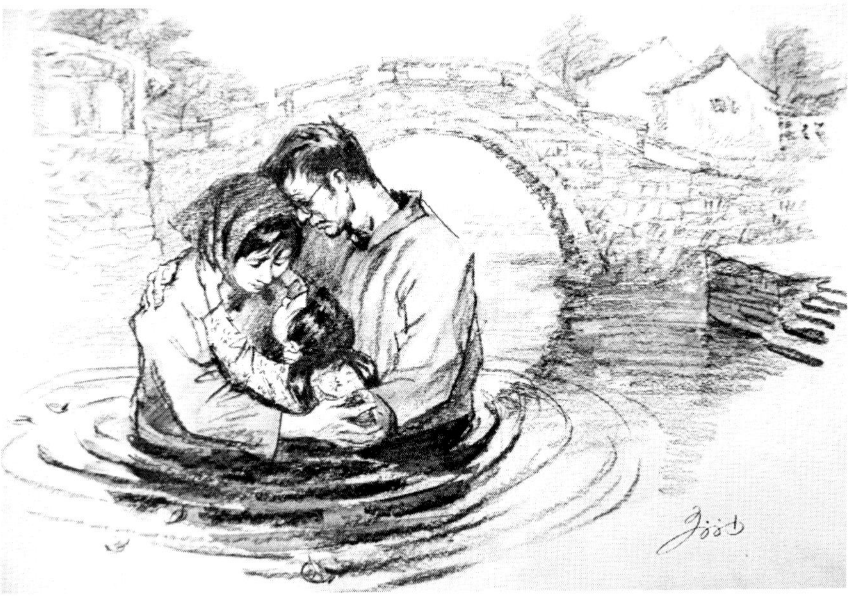

# Chapter 10.
## *Drowning In The River*

I don't remember how long we stood there. But my parents finally started to walk. Each of them held one of my hands and walked forward without saying a word for a long time. Eventually, we were outside the city. Broken pieces of coal and gravel began to pierce into my feet. I had lost both of my shoes while jumping off the horse earlier.

But I grit my teeth without a whimper because I was able to feel deeply the pain my parents were going through after losing my two brothers. Their feelings of sorrow, depression, and hopelessness was so thick that no words could adequately describe the atmosphere we were enshrouded in.

South of the city there was a river called the Dong An River. Over that river there was a bridge called Dong An Bridge. The three of us walked mechanically to the foot of the bridge. Mother gently let go of my hand and took a few steps ahead of us. She went to the middle of the bridge, which was also at the top and looked down at the water flowing under the arch of the bridge below her. I was not conscious of what Mother might be thinking, but Father rushed up to mother and quickly wrapped his arms around her.

He said, "No ! You cannot jump."

Mother turned and asked him, "Do we have any other choice?" She continued, "We have lost two sons with all of our meager belongings. Now Feng Huang (my name) has also lost her shoes.

## *The Memoir of a Six-Year-Old Refugee Girl*

Captain Tseng is gone, and the Japanese soldiers are close behind us. When they catch up with us we will surely die anyway. I might as well die here with some dignity left."

Father looked up in the sky and sighed deeply. He said, "All right, if that is the only choice then let us all die here together."

Mother leaned over to me and said, "Feng Huang, would you die with your father and me?"

When I was six years old, I had not thought about dying or even understood the meaning of it yet. But I was determined to follow my parents wherever they would go. So I answered without blinking my eyes, " Sure." Tears started to come down my cheeks, because I was still very scared of losing my parents. Mother cried. Father also cried.

Then Father led us down the bridge and walked to the edge of the shore lined with tall grass and weeds. My parents held hands and stared at each other for a while as if in a trance. Then they embraced together and rolled down the embankment into the river.
I saw Father pushing Mother's head into the water as he also submerged himself and
remained motionless. I followed them by walking into the water. It went over my knees and up to my waist.

When I took another step toward my parents the water went up to my chest, and I lost my footing. As I fell the water got up to my neck and I was scared. I screamed, "Mother! Dad! "
I saw Mother stirring. Then I felt a hand touching my leg in the water. It was my mother, who then grabbed hold of my leg as she raised her head above water. Mother was not dead. She almost became unconscious when she heard my cry. Her motherly instinct automatically motivated her into grabbing for my legs. The sensation of touching my leg woke her up and she raised her head. Fortunately the river was not very deep. It was only up to her neck while sitting down. She tugged at my father who also raised his

head and sat there breathing hard, choking out some of the water he had swallowed in the meantime. We looked at one another for a moment and then we all hugged one another into a heap and cried.

Mother struggled loose from our grip and said, "We cannot die. If we both die who would take care of our Feng Huang?"

At that statement, I cried even louder. So the three of us scrambled up the embankment and went back on the shore. We had no possessions. With the notion of dying behind us, my parents seemed relieved of a major burden. Since I had no shoes, my father decided to carry me on his shoulder until I got too heavy for him. Not much was said, but we felt a sense of belonging, an unspoken bond between us that was not there before. My parents seemed to have undergone a change of heart and were no longer afraid of anything. Years later they sometimes would talk about this experience at the Dong An River. To them it was their moment of awakening, a moment after which life or death, gain or loss, no longer seemed to matter to them. We were alive, and we just kept moving on.

# Chapter 11.
## *The Old Magistrate*

Now our family of five was left with only three people. None of us dared to mention the disappearance of my brothers for fear someone was going to cry. In the recent past, we had faced many scary moments and had escaped from numerous near-death crises. But each and every time, we had all five members of the family together. Something was missing from the spirit in the family sharing of life or death as a unit somehow.

We walked slowly and in total silence for a while. But on our way south, we did not meet another soul for a long time. Strange enough, the pursuing Japanese soldiers never did catch up with us. The scenery south of Dong An City on both sides of the highway was most beautiful. The flowery bushes, flowing rivers, and the background of green mountains were accentuated by the singing of the birds which presented us with a peaceful atmosphere that was in great contrast to a war-torn country full of refugees.

In earlier days, I used to fight and argue with my brothers for equal rights because male children used to come first in Hunan. Now I vowed a thousand times I would not fight with them ever again. I made up my mind I was going to pamper them if they would only come back. But we just maintained our pace all day going south. Several times in the afternoon, Mother would stop and call out for my brothers. When there was no answer from the countryside, she would then cry. Father and I would join her and we would end up crying in a heap. After a while we would again move on.

## Escape from Heng Yang:

I remember walking across a small wooden bridge and climbing over a fairly steep hill. By sundown we heard the barking of dogs and other noise coming from chickens and ducks. We knew we were getting close to people again. So we started to walk faster because our stomachs were growling with hunger. Soon we arrived at a large village that looked more like a small town with many houses built closely next to one another. We saw only one entrance to that village. There were several men standing guard near the entrance.

As we walked up to them, one of them leveled a musket pointing at my father and asked him: "Who are you? Stand still and be inspected."

We all stood in total shock.

Father raised his head to the sky and sighed deeply, " All right; all right! We have been inspected by the Japanese many times. Now we are even inspected by our own people. All this just because we did not wish to become second-class citizens. We ran away from the *Gui-Zi* and lost our sons. What do we have left for these people to inspect?" He raised his arms and walked up closer to that man and said, "Go ahead! Search me."

At that moment an older gentleman with long white beard and white hair came out from behind those men. His face was kind and gentle and he was dressed like a scholar. He pushed the musket aside from the first man and bowed deeply toward my father, " We are very sorry about all this." He said apologetically, " We have gathered the young men in our village in order to fight the Japanese invaders. There were many Chinese spies working for the Japanese so we need to be very careful in case they try to infiltrate into our village."

The old man continued, "Please forgive us. I am the magistrate of this county. After listening to what you just said, I know right away you cannot be a spy and you are no ordinary refugee. If you don't mind our humble dwelling, please come to my house for supper and stay with us for the night."

The mannerism of that old magistrate was sincere and very cordial. His language was also that of an educated person instead of a

## *The Memoir of a Six-Year-Old Refugee Girl*

farmer. So my parents quickly bonded with him and his people. That night we did stay at his big house. His people killed a chicken and a duck and cleaned some fish from the pond behind their house for dinner. It was a major feast and a bountiful dinner we would long remember. The magistrate inquired of my father while we ate as to why we had traveled so far away from our home in Heng Yang. Father told him everything that had happened. With tears, he told the magistrate how we lost my brothers on the way down. The old man also sighed with wet eyes as he heard our story.

After dinner they sat and had tea in the living room. The magistrate sat up straight while looking directly into my father's eyes and asked him, "Mr. Chen, I respect you for your grand decision to go to ChongQing. But have you ever thought of offering your service to the civilians who are left behind in the Japanese occupied territory?"

My father just shook his head in bewilderment.

So the old magistrate raised his two hands showing seven fingers as he said, "You see, Mr. Chen, the war against Japanese invasion since 1937 has been going on for seven years. None of us know just how long the fighting will go on. But we do have intelligence reports that the Japanese have reached Dong An. They will get to our village within a day or two at the latest. We have made some detailed plans." At this point he drew his chair closer toward my father and lowered his voice as if speaking to his confidant. The magistrate told my father that they had already moved all the women and children and old folks into large caverns in the mountain. I finally understood the absence of any women and children in the village. They had stored food and water in those caverns a couple of days trip away from the village. They would stop any small number of Chinese spies that might try to find their hiding place and tell the Japanese soldiers. They might even fight and kill any small number of Japanese sentries ahead of the main force. But as soon as the large group of Japanese soldiers came close, they would disappear into the mountains to hide for another day. He assured my father those caverns were quite secluded and were safe under their own armed guards far enough away from the main road. He told my father he was worried about the children in the village not

## Escape from Heng Yang:

getting a proper education in Chinese language and Chinese history. He was worried that the war might go on for another seven years. There was no one left to teach the children. He asked my father to consider staying with his people and be their teacher and school master.

Father looked at him with respect and showed surprise. He was lost for words for quite a while. The old magistrate patted him on the back and said gently, "Mr. Chen, why don't you and your family just stay with us for a while and see if this could work out?" Father became silent as he pondered the possibility. He was somewhat moved.

The magistrate continued after a sip of his tea, "You have already lost two sons. I sincerely pray and hope that nothing ever happens to the rest of your family. Besides, what if someone finds your two sons and happens to pass by our village? How can we get your sons to you if you keep on going?" The old magistrate was very persuasive and would have certainly changed the mind of just about anyone except my father who was real stubborn in his own right.

My father replied, "We have already paid a great price in order to escape out of the occupied territories in central Hunan. I can appreciate your kind invitation for us to stay. But if I had wanted to teach children in the occupied territory and be a second-class citizen to the Japanese *GuiZi*' I could have just stayed with my father in the Heng Yang countryside. No, my honorable magistrate sir, I thank you from the bottom of my heart. But to abandon our plan halfway would make all that effort seem worthless. I am sorry to disappoint you, but we must move on."

They continued their discussion into the wee hours of the night. But I soon lost interest in it and went to the next room and curled up next to my mother. I did not know if either of them ever went to bed that night. But the parting was quite cordial and friendly the next morning as the magistrate gave us water and food for the journey. He tried to give my father some money, but my father politely tried to refuse. Finally, Father took half of the stack of money and

## *The Memoir of a Six-Year-Old Refugee Girl*

vowed to send money back to the magistrate after we would arrive in Sichuan. The old magistrate looked disappointed. But he did not say another word.

Later as I grew older, I often remembered how that old magistrate stood at the entrance to his village with his white hair blowing in the wind as we walked farther away from him. China was fortunate to have patriotic magistrates like him who cared about people in their own villages and did not run away for their own lives in tough times.

So we continued to walk south along the highways of GuangXi. By early afternoon we arrived at another bigger village. This one was full of people and even had some shops in the village square. A man about my father's age was standing by the side of the road with his hand shielding the sun shining in his eyes and searching for something or someone in our direction. When he spotted us he quickly walked up to my father and asked: "Are you Mr. Chen, by any chance?" This unexpected familiarity caught Father totally by surprise.

But that man quickly put Father at ease when he identified himself as the son of the old magistrate whom we had just parted with that morning. As it turned out, this man operated a general store in the bigger village. His father, the old magistrate, had sent a messenger to him in the middle of the night about our arrival. So he again invited us to his house. My parents looked at each other and appeared greatly moved by his generosity on top of the magistrate's. To my own surprise, this time there was another little girl about my age at this gentleman's house!

Apparently since the first village in the north had served as a sentry post or a buffer in case of arrival by the Japanese soldiers, women and children were allowed to stay in this bigger village until they got a warning signal from the north.

Once more we were given the kind of hospitality any sojourner could have ever dreamed of. The young daughter of our host and

## Escape from Heng Yang:

hostess and I quickly became the best of friends. Her mother gave me a complete girl's outfit which she had ordered custom made by the village tailor shop for her daughter. She also gave me a pair of shoes that was exactly my size! I heard the host saying to my father what the old magistrate had told him through the messenger that it was a great misfortune of these villages and the entire county to lose a good teacher like my father. Under the circumstances, Father looked at Mother for a long time without saying a word.

When Father slapped his hand on the table, he startled all of us, especially my new little friend and I. Father exclaimed, "All right! Thanks to you and your father's sincerity and your hospitality, we will stay here for a while and will try to teach the children."

Our host and his wife smiled with their mouths grinning from ear to ear. Everyone was happy.

So we stayed in this village as father managed to start the school on the very next day in a one-room school house. My little friend and I joined four or five other children in the first grade class. Father also taught another class for some older children about ten to twelve years old. Somehow the villagers found half of a wood board for the classroom. Father used a brush to write the lessons on large white sheets of paper with good Chinese calligraphy and hung them on that wood board. We copied the lessons on our own sheets of paper with lead pencils because brushes made of bamboo sticks and lamb's wool or wolf's hair were hard to come by during the war years. The lessons went on for several days. But I could sense father's mood in the evenings when the children all went home.

He became restless again after just three or four days. Apparently with the approaching Japanese soldiers not too far behind us, the thought of losing our freedom again as second-class citizens once more ignited Father's will to move on. Despite the friendly persuasion of the son of the old magistrate, we finally said goodbye to our host and hostess and my newfound little friend.

Was it an act of God or was it just fate that we stayed in that

## *The Memoir of a Six-Year-Old Refugee Girl*

area for four more days ? We would never know for sure. But strange things were about to befall upon us.

# Chapter 12.
## *Ride The Refugee Train To GuiLin*

I don't know if other children my age ever had the privilege to ride on a refugee train. But how can anyone ever forget such a unique experience?

After we left the second village in the old magistrate's county, we had to climb over another deserted mountain. But this time as we reached the top of the mountain, we saw a railway station and a refugee train parked along the open-air platform of the train station. It was a sight I can still remember today when I close my eyes.

There were people riding on top of the train since all the railroad cars were full. Then there were people lying on boards fastened to the body frame of the train from below the railroad cars! ! This train was stuffed and fully covered with people. But we were thinking about the alternative to walking on foot. Riding on the train, we could save so much time in our long journey to ChongQing that we waved to the train conductor as we ran toward the train station. Our legs carried us toward the train almost as if by some magical and automatic movement that we forgot the pain. By the time we all climbed on top of one of the last railroad cars, we were totally out of breath! We ended up holding onto the ropes strung across the top of the train for our safety as we rode in the "upper class." We would later enjoy the sunshine along with the fast wind and some rain as we traveled. We had to crouch down low or lie flat on our stomachs as the train went through some tunnels. A few of our fellow passengers fell asleep, lost their grips, and fell off the train and were never heard of again. Father tied a thinner

## *The Memoir of a Six-Year-Old Refugee Girl*

rope around my waist just in case. Mother held onto the rope with one of her hands while hanging onto my other hand for dear life. My free hand held onto the rope next to me all the time. Occasionally I had to change hands with Mother to allow blood flow. But we managed to survive the ride.

In the "middle class" of the train it was a regular sardine factory. Not only were the seats fully occupied with people, many children were lying flat on the luggage racks overhead on both sides of each railroad car. People fell asleep while standing and leaning on one another with no room to spare in the aisles. Oftentimes the children could not wait to go to the restroom so they simply had accidents in the pants. There was no room for anyone to move forward or backward in those railroad cars, let alone trying to reach the restrooms at each end. Besides, those restrooms were also fully occupied with passengers. Those restrooms simply consist of oblong holes in the floor. There were many wounded soldiers and sick and elderly who had "priority" seats in the "middle class" railroad cars. Smells of sweat, urine, and decayed food permeated throughout those railroad cars!

The under class was the most difficult to explain to a stranger. It was also the most unimaginable by people whose own country had never been massively attacked by other nations leading to refugee lives for millions. Wood boards were somehow mounted under every train car between the train axels. Then the people (mostly adults) would lie flat on those boards as the train moved rapidly forward over the tracks. One of their hands would hang onto a rope run between the axels while the other hand would hold onto their bags of belongings. At any time if they rolled off the boards, they would be ground into a pulp by the iron wheels. So at that time I thought we were lucky to have found three "seats" in the "upper class."

One of the unpleasant things we discovered to our dismay was that the train was running on a low grade of coal and the soot permeated through the chimney blowing by all of us the whole time. Soon we were not only covered with the soot but were coughing incessantly, almost choking to death until the wind somehow carried the exhaust over our heads at a higher level to spare us. But the train was no longer running on schedule. It stopped whenever it was low on coal or water. It stopped below the hills when it became steep for such a heavily loaded train. Occasionally the train engineer would release a car or two from the rear to lessen its load going uphill. A huge commotion would result as those unfortunate ones would scramble into or over the cars ahead of them. Many often were then left behind to fend for themselves. So we stopped, moved, stopped again from morning to evening, from night into dawn.

Sometimes, when Mother thought about my two brothers she would sob quietly and I would encircle her with my two arms while Father would clutch onto one of her arms real tight. The three of us stayed together on top of the train or on the ground on stops to relieve ourselves or to find something to eat. There was not a chance we would again be separated. The train was progressing very slowly. Father mumbled once or twice that if we had walked, we might have arrived in GuiLin already. But we stayed with the train mostly because Mother's injuries to her feet were not yet healed and because my own blisters and cuts from the long journey were taking their toll. We thought we'd never get to GuiLin. Then a miracle happened!

One morning the train stopped as if it was going to stay a very long time. So I asked Father if we could get off to stretch our legs because mine were numb. We all got off and walked along the length of the train just in case the engineer would decide to take off at any time.

We heard a faint yell, "Mr. Chen!" and turned to look. Then a man appeared from the top of one of the train cars, yelling at my father while waving his right arm feverishly. "Mr. Chen!" He was wearing a Chinese soldier's uniform.

We walked rapidly toward the train to find out what was going on. His left arm was in a sling, appearing to have been injured. With great excitement, he yelled to my father, " I am from Captain Tseng's unit. The captain wants you to join him immediately,

## *The Memoir of a Six-Year-Old Refugee Girl*

because he has found your two sons!" Looking at my father's bewildered face, he added, " Go to GuiLin. Go to GuiLin. That's where he is." He pointed his finger in the direction of GuiLin.

At first my parents were totally stunned at hearing the news. But after a moment of astonishment, they jumped up and down with joy. "Really? Did you see our boys? How are they? Where are they? And where is Captain Tseng?"

The soldier tossed a canteen of water to my father and said with equal excitement, "Your boys are just fine. They are with Captain Tseng who just left with them for GuiLin this morning. You should find them if you hurry."

At this point, I also got excited and jumped up and down.

My parents looked at each other and looked at the refugee train, which was stopped dead in its tracks. Tears of joy flowed freely down their cheeks as they each held onto one of my hands while yelling at the messenger of great news, " *Xie, Xie* (Thanks)! *Xie, Xie*!" Then the three of us turned and ran toward GuiLin like three crazy people.

# Chapter 13.
## *My First Marathon to…Oh, My Brothers!*

The three of us ran and stopped for breath and ran again until none of us could run any longer. We leaned against a tree on the side of the road to rest for a while. Then after a few minutes, we started to run again, forgetting all the pains in our feet and our ankles. Sometimes my parents were running so fast my feet barely touched the ground as they dragged me forward. We took sips from the canteen of water as we made stops. But we ran and ran. From early morning until noon, we finally saw the city gate of GuiLin. We were astonished as we entered the city because we saw no civilians in the city. Only soldiers and officers of various Chinese army units occupied the city. It reminded us of DongAn.

So my parents tried to ask every officer or soldier we encountered, " Do you know where we can find Captain Tseng of xx regiment ?"
"I don't know!" was the usual reply.
No one seemed to know who or where Captain Tseng was.
Then one of the officers asked my father, "Who the xxx are you? Why would a civilian ask about an army officer?"
Just as Father was trying to explain to him, we heard a familiar voice shouting from a quarter of a kilometer away, " Mr. Chen, Mr. Chen!"
So we all turned around.

We saw a tall officer running toward us in huge strides as he shouted my father's name. We all jumped up and down with great

## *The Memoir of a Six-Year-Old Refugee Girl*

joy as we recognized Captain Tseng! Father ran toward him with extended hands and got a huge bear hug. His tears came streaming down as if the captain had been our closest relative!

"*Tai Hao Le! Tai Hoa Le* (Too good to be true)!" exclaimed Captain Tseng. "You arrived here just in time, because I had almost given up ever seeing you again. I was going to bring your two sons to my old home in the countryside to let my wife take care of them as my own children until the end of the war. If you guys did not get here until tomorrow you might not see them for a very long time."

Mother yelled out: "Are they all right? Where did you find them? Were they not injured?"

"Those two little guys are robust and strong," exclaimed the captain. He asked, " So you want to know how the heck we found them?

" As you might know, we had thought that those two *tiao fu* had fallen behind our group." He continued, "but they had actually gone way in front of us in Dong An City. And when they realized that they were no longer being watched, they simply chose to take off without the two boys."

Father said, "I guess since my father had paid them half of the wages ahead of time
and since they knew we were running short of money they figured they might not collect the second half for a very long time anyway."

Captain Tseng said, "It was a good thing that I chose the narrower road instead of the main highway out of Dong An City or we would have missed them."

He added, "Lieutenant Wang heard some kids crying from afar and went over to check them out. The two boys were sitting in the dirt next to a dry well and the younger one was crying as Lieutenant Wang approached them. They thought you guys didn't want them anymore!"

Mother, with happy tears streaming down, said, "Oh, no. How could we ever abandon our two beloved sons?"

Father and I also nodded as our tears of joy came unstopped.

Captain Tseng said, "I had sent a couple of riders back to Dong An trying to find you guys, but I guess they must have missed you on the way. So I thought if we could not find you, I would keep them until the end of the war. Then I'd advertise in all the major newspapers until I would find you again. And if I could not find you, I would just raise them as if they were my own children."

There were simply no words that could adequately describe our appreciation for Captain Tseng for what he had done for us. Even as young as I was, I could sense the deeply heart-felt gratitude from my parents. Then in a very tiny house in a muddy yard, we finally saw my two brothers again!

As soon as XiaoDi saw my mother, he sprang across the room and went "Wa!" With huge drops of tears, he buried himself in her bosom while Mother clutched him real tight. QiLing, my twin, had a toy gun in his hand, probably given to him by Lieutenant.Wang. When he saw us with his swollen red eyes, he pursed his lips and raised the toy gun at us and said, "Bang, Bang! Why have you abandoned us?"

Father ran over and embraced QiLing in his arms as I joined them in a huge embrace. We all laughed and cried in a big heap as Captain Tseng looked on and nodded his head in broad smiles of approval. The reunion was a bittersweet experience unequaled in any future experiences I would ever encounter in the rest of my life.

Then, in a very emotional state, my parents dragged the three of us children and knelt in front of Captain Tseng to express our sincere gratitude to our benefactor.

As it turned out, we had been separated from my two brothers for a total of seven whole days. Thinking back on the refugee lives in those days, to be able to reunite with one's family in chaos after seven long days was unimaginable, and it was a real miracle.

Later when we had time to sit down and chat, we found out that they had just arrived in GuiLin a few hours before us. If we had not met that soldier on the refugee train earlier and did our marathon run to GuiLin, we would have simply missed them.

Was it fate that we encountered that kind old magistrate? Was it fate that kept us in the small town where his son and his family lived? Was it fate that we stayed in that town for three days instead of four? Was it fate that sent my crying sound into my mother's ears as my parents almost drowned themselves in the river? Was it fate that we rode that refugee train and got to meet that wounded soldier from Captain Tseng's unit?

Thus, early in my life, I learned when people missed one another by a few minutes or by a few feet, they could end up being separated thousands of kilometers apart from one another. Although I never belonged to any religious group the rest of my life, I do believe in fate. I have heard people say life is made up of a large string of happenings. And as the story of this reunion with my two brothers shall testify, a strange but wonderful fate did fall upon my beloved family.

It was a great fortune that we encountered Captain Tseng, the miracle worker.

# Chapter 14.
## *Goodbye, Captain Tseng !*

After finding my brothers in GuiLin (GuangXi), we were told to leave the city as soon as possible because all the retreating units of the Chinese army from other cities in central China had ended up in GuiLin, and all of us civilians had to leave to make room for them all. The five hundred thousand Japanese troops dispatched in their assignment for the number one takeover battle (*Yi Hao Zuo Zhan*) of central China had been proven to be truly devastating for the poorly equipped Chinese defensive forces in Hunan province, my home. Sooner or later there was going to be a major battle in GuiLin, we were told.

During our last two days in GuiLin my parents held numerous meetings with captain Tseng. At one of those meetings, my bothers and I went through a most solemn ceremony in the Chinese custom, recognizing Captain Tseng as our "Dry Father" (similar to godfather in Western tradition). We had to kneel in front of him three times, each time we knocked our heads on the ground three times.

Although we had anticipated traveling with Captain Tseng through GuiZhou Province and perhaps all the way to ChongQing, at the last minute he received an order to stay in GuiLin and "fight until the last man." So he arranged for us to go forward while he organized his men, horses, and equipment in Guilin for the final fight against the Japanese invaders. Then he came to say goodbye to us. He was very positive about meeting us in ChongQing after the Chinese army would chase the *GuiZi* back out of our country.

## *The Memoir of a Six-Year-Old Refugee Girl*

    I don't know exactly how my parents felt about Captain Tseng. But I had already developed a strong feeling toward him as if he were my own father. Whether it got started when he held me close with his big arm around me on his big horse or when I saw him sharing his canteen water with me and my family until it was all gone, I will never know. But how could I ever thank him enough for finding my brothers after losing touch with them for seven whole days? But all good things must come to an end. We finally had to say goodbye to Captain Tseng.

    Captain Tseng had some of his men occupying a "square" for us in the refugee train going out of Guilin in the westerly direction. It consisted of two benches in one of the "middle class" cars, but none of my family had to either ride on top of the train or lie flat on a board between the grinding iron wheels. When he led us into our "square," I also saw our old luggage, which his men had found when they had discovered my brothers by the dry well. So after giving me a bear hug, Captain Tseng said goodbye to the rest of my family and got off the train. I pressed my nose tightly against the train window as the train started to move. Tears began to roll down my cheeks as I frantically tried to wave at Captain Tseng. Father raised the train window so we could stick our heads out to wave at him. Then the train moved faster and faster. The tall and handsome figure on the platform began to diminish as we moved, until finally it became just a small dot. Father closed the window with a deep sigh. My tears came right back again as I said softly, "Goodbye."

    It was the very last time we saw Captain Tseng. Throughout the rest of our journey, we tried to find information about his unit in the Chinese army as we encountered other soldiers who had participated in the final defense of GuiLin city. All we learned was that the city was overrun by more than two hundred thousand Japanese soldiers after many days of bombardment to soften it up. No one could give us any information regarding Captain Tseng or his men. In fact, after the war was over in September 1945, my parents put ads in the newspapers all over China to no avail. It became a permanent regret of my family for not finding him.

# Escape from Heng Yang:

According to the plan my parents had made with Captain Tseng, we were to go west on the train from GuiLin and then go north through GuiZhou province to Sichuan. I was never told why, but soon we got off the train and started to walk again. Every one of us had to walk with a package on our backs, myself included. We walked as much as ten to fifteen kilometers a day. All I could remember was the huge number of refugees walking next to us. They filled all the nooks and crannies in those treacherous mountain roads we traveled. There were old folks and young babies being carried. Many years later I saw the movie *Ten Commandments*, starring Charleton Heston. The scene with all the Israelite refugees walking out of Egypt very much resembled the crowd we were in. But our Exodus out of GuiLin had neither ducks nor geese walking alongside. If any of them had been herded along, they would have become dinner long before we reached GuiZhou Province.

My four-year-old brother cried a lot. But after missing them for seven long days even his crying was lovely music to me. At least our family was now together. The sense of peace and relief in our family reunion was probably not shared by too many other refugee families. Not far west of Guilin we started to walk northward to GuiZhou.

The little bit of money given to us by the old magistrate and his son was long gone. Overruling my parents' objections, Captain Tseng had stuffed some money into my father's hands before he left us on the train out of GuiLin. But by the time we arrived in Rong Shui, the seat of Rong County in northern GuangXi Province, Mother declared that we were out of cash again. Rong Shui was rather large, but by the time we got there, it was already full of refugees.

# Chapter 15.
## *Malaria? Oh, Mother!*

The county seat of Rong was a rather large town. By that time it was already filled with refugees from other parts of China. Father found a pawn shop on the main street and exchanged everything of value for cash. Mother also gingerly submitted her last piece of jewelry, a very small gold ring (somehow she was able to conceal it), for money that would carry us through just a couple more days. Then she fell ill just at that worst of times.

In those days without DDT to control the mosquitoes, malaria was rampant around GuangXi and GuiZhou, especially among the refugees who had no money to buy food, let alone buying and carrying mosquito nets with them. A malaria patient usually alternates between fever and chills at least once every other day. But the particular type from GuiZhou occurred once every day. It was worse than other strains of malaria when it hit. And it took a much longer time before the patient recovered. During those days of poor and unpredictable living conditions, many refugees died of malaria and lack of proper care or food. Local people called it *Da Bai Zi*, describing the condition of the patient between fever and chills. Upon hearing it, everyone would exhibit fear upon their faces, because sometimes it lasts many years before it would go away. The miracle drug for malaria was Quinine which was in short supply during WWII, so it was extremely expensive. As the Chinese saying goes, "A leaky house gets hit with continuous rain." My mother finally came down with the GuiZhou strain of malaria in the tiny hotel room when we were totally out of money and resources.

# Escape from Heng Yang:

No money, no medicine, no food. There were neither friends nor relatives in Rong County. Mother was lying in bed, whimpering all day long. My father ran around town with some old clothes for cash attempting to buy a few Quinine pills. So I became the official care person for my mother at the age of six. I would wring the cold wet towel for her when she had a fever. Then when she got the chills, I would bring her a hot towel dripping wet from the boiling hot kettle, while making sure she did not get burned. I could never forget the fearful sense of death and abandonment encroaching upon us while my father was gone.

One morning as I was there waiting on my mother in between her fever and chills, I felt dizzy in my head since the only thing I had in my stomach was one bowl of very diluted rice gruel given to me by my father before he left. Then Mother stopped her whimpering, opened her eyes wide, and said in a whisper to me, "What would you kids do if I should die?"

At this point I could no longer hold it in and cried, "Oh, Ma!" and went "Wah!" My tears flowed like a river that would not stop. Mother became really scared and held me in her arms trying to comfort me and to calm me down. But my eyes were like broken levees, forming a flooded river. I was like a torrential outbreak as I kept on crying until I passed out into a heap.

When I woke up, there was a cold towel on my forehead, and a stranger was standing there looking down at me. Later I learned he was our doctor. It finally dawned on me that I was also hit by malaria. Along with the fever and chills, I also had a horrible headache and pains all over my body. I sweated all over with the fever and headache; I shook like a leaf as the chills hit me. My teeth would hit like a chatter box. This illness stayed with me for many years until I was in high school.

So two out of five in my family collapsed with malaria. We owed rent money to the hotel, medical bills to the doctor and to the pharmacy. The hotel owner was afraid we might die in his hotel

## *The Memoir of a Six-Year-Old Refugee Girl*

room so he was willing to forsake the money we owed him as long as we moved on. Since the conversation between my parents often touched on hopelessness and death, I began to think about the times when the three of us almost drowned ourselves in the river at Dong An. Why did we not die then? Why did we later find my brothers alive? Would another miracle ever happen again?

One morning my mother and I were both whimpering in bed while my twin brother was there to hand us the cold and hot towels with my father gone again in the streets to try to find a way out for us. Suddenly the door to our hotel room burst open. A strange young man followed Father into the tiny room.

My father yelled out, "See whom I just ran into in the streets of Rong County?"

That young man quickly came over to Mother and said, "*Shi-Mu Ning Hao*?" (*Shi-Mu* is the respectful address for the wife of one's teacher; Lao-Shi was for the teacher in the old days.) He continued, "What a terrible situation you people have ended up in this town!"

As it turned out, Mr. Xiao was one of my father's favorite students back in Heng Yang. At the time he ran into my father, he was a teaching assistant and a graduate student at GuangXi University in Nan-Ning. The university had just been closed for a few days and was trying to move its administration office and files and some books to a more rural location. They ended up in Rong County where we were staying. Mr. Xiao ran into my father while my father was walking aimlessly from one street to another in Rong.

Very quickly, Mr. Xiao went to the hotel owner and paid up what we had owed. Then he paid the doctor, the pharmacy, and bought food for us from the market. His generosity and his quick action without a moment of hesitation won deep affection and gratitude from all of us. Thus, as if it were pre-arranged by some unknown forces, our family was once more miraculously rescued out of a desperate situation.

With help from Mr. Xiao, we received the much-needed medi-

## Escape from Heng Yang:

cine--Quinine for our malaria infection and the much-needed food to keep us alive and well. In order to set up our financial sufficiency, Mr. Xiao then introduced my father to the head of the administration of the exiled GuangXi University in Rong county. At that time most of the regular teaching staff of the university had either gone home to rural countryside or had gone forward to Guiyang , the capitol of GuiZhou Province. Only a few teachers/and professors came with their family to travel with the administration staff. The dean of academic affairs, being uncertain of enough good quality teachers when they traveled toward their final destiny in Guiyang, decided to give my father an offer to teach with a reduced salary during our trip. Father was happy to accept anything at that point and it was settled.

Therefore, as a result of my mother's illness in Rong County, my father got a job and we stayed temporarily in Rong County until the exiled GuangXi University started to travel again.

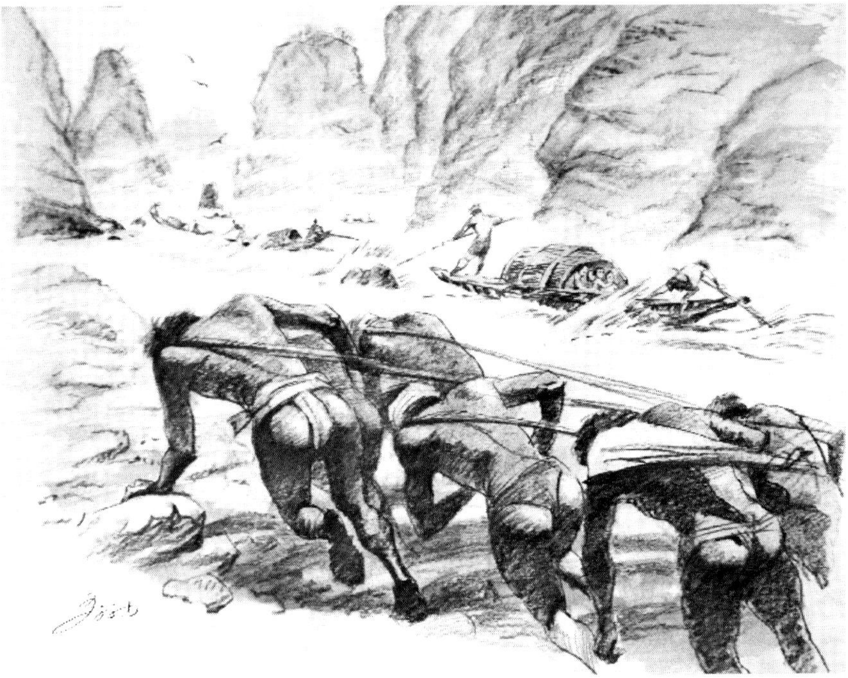

# Chapter 16.
## *Twenty Days in RongHe River*

One day, the exiled GuangXi University administration staff plus my family all boarded more than twenty small *sampans* (covered boats). Each *sampan* had to accommodate two families if not loaded with boxes of files or books. In the center of the *sampan* was hung a bed sheet to separate the two families. So we were packed like sardines with some of us exposed to the weather elements. Fortunately as a result of us traveling upstream, we were not going too fast so no one fell off the boat as a result of the rowing during level portions of the river or the tortuous pole-pushing by the boatman in fast-flowing waters. In the daytime, we sat around our half of the *sampan* under the bamboo cover. But at night, someone had to take turns being extended outside of the cover while we all tried to sleep lying down. I was the oldest child in the family, so it was my turn to be exposed outside the cover most of the time. This arrangement was bearable on a clear day, but when it rained three days out of five on the river, it was hard not to get soggy and become chilled to the bones at night. Thus, it was another one among many miracles in our refugee days that I did not get seriously ill. Malaria did not come back to haunt me more than once on the river journey, thanks to the remaining few Quinine pills.

Our breakfast usually consisted of rice gruel with a bit of brown sugar. Lunch was rice with salty pickles with some dried fish caught by the boatman in the river. A special favorite dish, which we were happy to partake once every two days was a small bottle of soy beans sautéed by my mother that was smothered in spicy hot peppers. It was so special that each of us only received a few kernels each time. I usually would savor these few kernels of soy beans in my mouth for quite a long time before finally chewing them up and swallowing them along with my rice.

One day when our *sampan* was moored at another river port, some villagers came by to sell their cooked corn-on-the-cobs. The smell of steamed corn-on-the-cob was so enticing to small children that we continuously begged our parents to buy one for us. Under the circumstances at that time, a corn-on-the-cob was considered a luxury item that was way out of our family budget limits. But after some noisy whining by the three of us, my father finally gave in and allowed Mother to buy one for us to share. So we counted and divided those corn kernels as if they were real pearls. Even today, I can still remember the delicious flavor of that one ear of corn.

Our *sampan* was operated by a father-and-son team. The son was merely a teenager, not much taller than me at the time. So one might count them as a one-and-a-half man team. Portions of the RongHe River, however, were quite fast-flowing during the rainy season. Looking at the map much later, I found we had traveled in a twisted fashion from northern GuangXi into south-eastern GuiZhou region in a north-westerly direction. Sometimes there were high mountains on both sides of the river so even with both father and son at the poles pushing with all their might, we were moving very slow along one side of the river bank. Understandably, they could operate only in daytime hours and would drop anchor at night because of all the submerged rocks near the shore. Had they tried to go upstream in the middle of the river, the *sampan* would have been carried backward by the swift current. In order not to be scattered by the river current in the night, all twenty *sampans* were held together by ropes before everyone went to sleep.

On those nights we anchored along deserted shores with higher banks, everyone just stayed in his or her *sampan*. But whenever we anchored near a town or village, everyone was always glad to go on shore. The adults would go hunt for food or other supplies, while

## Escape from Heng Yang:

we played with whatever we could find.

One early evening while I strolled along the shore I found a couple of lovely white stones that had smooth surfaces. One of the uncles in the convoy told me they were "fire stones" that would give sparks of fire when one struck them against each other. So I learned to strike them in the dark to make beautiful sparks. Soon I became a collector of stones. To my amazement, some of those pretty stones gave colors of red, green, or orange, but mostly just yellow. Playing with those stones did help to pass time when there was nothing exciting for us along the way.

One morning after breakfast, I played with my stone collection at the bow of our *sampan* before we got started. Suddenly the *sampan* was hit by one of those fast rotating "twisters" in the river current and I was thrown into the river! The river current where we had dropped anchor the night before had been quite slow. But during the night, there was a steady rain and our *sampan* rose by two feet in the morning as the river became widened by more water. Fortunately the father operator of our *sampan* was washing the rice bowls at the rear end of the boat. He quickly dove into the river after me and grabbed hold of my hair. Then, with a couple of fast kicks of his legs in the water, he pushed both of us toward the shore. If it had not been for him being there, I would have been surely drowned in the RongHe River. As it turned out, I only had to swallow a couple of mouthfuls.

But I cried and cried as my mother gathered me in her lap to comfort me. When I finally calmed down, I told her I was all right. I was merely crying over my pretty stone collection. Since I lost my small silk flag in that village fire set by the Japanese soldiers near HengYang, I had not cried so hard over any other treasures for a long time. Over the course of our long trip on the river, I witnessed other people falling into the river when they were careless as they did their daily "business" while squatting near the edge of the boat. Oftentimes, someone would grab hold of the hair of a fallen victim (especially if it were a child) and pulled him or her out of the water.

## *The Memoir of a Six-Year-Old Refugee Girl*

But once in a while, we lost one among the twenty *sampans* in the middle of the night when no one was watching. Thus, I learned in my early childhood that buoyancy of the water and human hair could work as lifesavers.

A couple of days later my lifesaver, the father of our *sampan* team, fell ill with a severe recurrence of malaria, which he had contracted a year before meeting us. Even with his lean and muscular body and all his seemingly boundless energy and iron will, he was knocked flat by the fevers and chills carried by a tiny insect! So with the father being out of commission while we were out of Quinine pills, the upstream maneuvering of our *sampan* fell on the shoulders of his teenage son. The progress of our *sampan* became slower and slower until we were completely separated from the rest of the *sampan* convoy. We sometimes were merely drifting in swift current downstream. So with the help of my father and the father of the second family we managed to get to the shore. The father-owner of the *sampan* tied our boat to a rock and went ashore to buy some medicine as his son became our captain for a day. The owner left us in such a hurry that he forgot to drop anchor for a more secured stop.

After some time, the powerful swift current somehow jiggled the rope loose from the rock and we started drifting downstream! The boy captain tried everything he knew to steady the *sampan*. At the end, he tried to pull on some long weeds on the shore while every adult on the boat tried to grab on something to stop the *sampan* from drifting away. Just as we all were going to lose grip or hope the father-owner came back! He double-tied the *sampan* to a tree on shore with a long rope and dropped anchor as the day drew to an end. His son helped my mother make rice for supper. So we stayed overnight at an unscheduled location. The next morning at the crack of dawn, even when I was still asleep, our *sampan* team already started rowing and pushing the poles upstream. Our *sampan* team overcame the stretch of swift current and finally managed to catch up with the rest of the *sampan* convoy just as they finished with their breakfast and were about to get started for the day. The people from the rest of the convoy were very amazed we were able to catch up with them, because two other *sampans* that had lost their ways early on had not caught up with the rest of the group.

After this horrifying drifting experience in the river, we found ourselves able to manage just about any more inconvenience and pains during the rest of the trip. Our confidence level was greatly increased and we no longer envied those "rich" people who traveled upstream in those large passenger boats. Each of those boats were pulled on shore by a team of coolies whenever they were going through a stretch of swift current such as the one we had just encountered. There were men at the poles as well. They all took up the oars in more level stretches of water.

But it was worth noting that the coolies on the shore would sing their rope-pulling tunes in a rhythmic fashion with the leader yelling in a higher pitched voice, "*Way*.... Yo-Oh" and the rest of them answering in a much lower pitched: "*Hai*....Yo-Oh" as they struggled forward with the long rope on their back glistening with sweat in the sun light. This was also true with the cargo boats. Their singing cries were slightly musical but were filled with the sadness of survival with a throaty roar from generations of long suffering history. People who rode in those large boats had a lot of money. They based their comfort on the pain and suffering of others, I thought.

Later when I was in high school in Taiwan I learned a song named: "The Rope-pulling Boatmen" that went as follows:

> Again and again as we move forward,
> Everyone holding onto a part (of the rope);
> With our eyes fixed upon our Headman,
> Our strong wills unaltered by any swift current!
> In the midst of terrific waves and dangerous swells
> We manage to calmly and leisurely pull the boat onward;
> We always manage to arrive (at our destiny)
> From seemingly endless long trips;
> Whether we are heading toward
> North, South, East or West !

## *The Memoir of a Six-Year-Old Refugee Girl*

The lyrics were quite happy and the music was loud and with high spirit. But the part about "calmly and leisurely pull the boat onward in the midst of ….. swells" was very different from what I remembered as a child. The boat-pulling coolies of yesterday had no leisure and calm in their struggle to survive. Perhaps the tune from the "Volga River Boatmen" might have been much more appropriate.

Eventually we managed to settle down in our routine in that crowded *sampan*. After three weeks in the RongHe River, we finally arrived at Rongjiang City in GuiZhou province. Rongjiang, however, was not our destiny. We still had a long way to travel to ChongQing.

# Chapter 17.
## *Father Sells Yams*

When our group arrived in Rongjiang, GuiZhou Province, we were told that the financial conditions of the exiled GuangXi University was far worse than the treasurer had anticipated. Due to no more funding from the also exiled ministry of education then in ChongQing (the temporary capital during WWII) and no more tuition being received from students (no classes and no students) the university on the move had simply run out of money. So even a partial salary to my father who had yet to teach one single class got suspended indefinitely.

Thus, it was everyone for himself as most of the group from the twenty *sampans* were dispersed, heading in all directions. We said our goodbyes to all the families and friends, especially to Mr. Xiao, who had saved our family from a terrible mess. He made sure that we could travel on our own and proceeded to move some of the university possessions with the administrative staff westward to Guiyang while we continued going north toward Chongqing. Staying alive, to be sure, was our main objective.

There were several native tribes in GuiZhou including the Miao and the Shui. But the one tribe which was the predominant one around the southeastern region of GuiZhou was the Dong tribe. Their favorite food was a pan-fried cake made of stone-ground sticky rice flour. It was called *Ci-Ba* (*Ci* sounds like *Tsi*). The second favorite one was the sweet potato or yam. But since I could never tell them apart, I would call them all yams. During winter of

## *The Memoir of a Six-Year-Old Refugee Girl*

1944-45, walking around while holding a hot steamed or baked yam in my two little hands and taking small bites out of it was a great enjoyment!

After a brief discussion with Mother, Father took most of his meager severance pay from the exiled GuangXi University and invested in a bag of sticky rice flour and some oil for mother to make *Ci-Ba* while buying a pot and some raw yams for himself, plus a Chinese GanCheng (weighing stick). It was made of a long, smooth, wooden stick with many dots painted on it away from the fulcrum where a very strong piece of rope was fixed through a hole on the stick. At the short end of the stick was a hook for hanging the pan or simply for hooking onto whatever was to be weighed. Along the long end of the stick hung an iron weight, which can be placed at certain locations on the long stick to balance the object being weighed. Large dots on the stick indicated divisions for *Jin* (about a pound) while the smaller dots between every two large dots would indicate *Liang* (about an ounce). So my mother would fry and sell Ci-Ba with the help of my twin brother and would keep an eye on my XiaoDi. Father took me to the corner of a street intersection to cook and sell yams from the pot.

At the time in Rongjiang City there were tens of thousands of refugees like us. There were at least a dozen people at the same street corner selling yams. Although my father could teach in classrooms about ancient Chinese history for hours, he was like a *MuJi* (wooden rooster) standing at that street corner selling yams.

Unlike the other people trying to hawk their yams at passers by, my father was a gentleman in sales. A Chinese saying dating back to a prime minister of HanWenDi, the king, named *Jiangtaigong* goes like this: "*YuenZheShangGou*" ( *Jiangtaigong* used to go fishing without worms on his hook–only the fish which was willing to be caught would get on the hook). So no one approached us until all the other yam sellers were sold out. Then a man came by to buy half of a *Jin* of yams. So Father happily opened the lid and tried to scoop up some steamy hot yams in the pot. It took him a while to drain the liquid off and wrapped them up in a clean, white, paper wrap cone. Then he placed the wrapped yams in the pan and picked up the fulcrum on the *GanCheng*. He balanced the pan by moving the iron weight on the long stick.

Turning to me, he said, "FengHuang, where does it say half of a *Jin*?" My father was very near-sighted so while holding that GanCheng up straight, it was difficult for him to read it without bending down.

But as a six-year-old barely able to read a few Chinese characters and count to a hundred it was difficult for me to stretch my neck up and read the dots on that weighing stick correctly. No one had trained me on the *GanCheng* so I remember standing there with my father, both of us with faces as red as the yams. The owner at the next pot felt sorry for my father and came over to help us determine that the wrapped yams weighed a little more than half of a *Jin*. But as my father was about to remove the package from the pan under the *GanCheng*, it tipped over. The entire paper-wrapped yams fell to the ground in a messy heap!

Sensing that the only buying customer was getting to the end of his patience, my father threw the *GanCheng* on the ground, opened the lid to the pot and said: " Fine, just take as much as you'd like from my pot."

That man took and wrapped some yams, handed some money to my red-faced father and left. Thus, that only transaction ended our yams selling business career.

How my mother had fared with her sales of *Ci-Ba* I had no clue. But in the next several days, our daily meals consisted either of steaming hot yams or of *Ci-Ba*.

Somehow we encountered another family headed by Uncle Zhai. The Zhai family was the same size as ours except there were three girls in the family. Uncle Zhai felt the same way about walking all the way to Chongqing as my father so that we decided to travel together. Mrs. Zhai and my mother hit it off quite well, thinking that we could all help to look after one another in a group.

Uncle Zhai said to my father, "The children can play with one another while we adults can talk as we walk. Before you know it, we'll be there in Chongqing."

Uncle Zhai told us about his many ways to make money. He said, "With all my many skills in making money, we will never starve." He also had a special talent in doing the *JinGangjing* (the Diamond chant) which was derived from the *DaBeiZhou* (the great Odes of Empathy from Buddha) that supposedly could turn a crisis into a peaceful and tranquil situation. He claimed that by reciting the *JinGangJing* he could cure almost all ills, unless an unfaithful nonbeliever would dare to counter his chant.

I don't remember other details while traveling with the Zhai family anymore. But there was never a dull moment while we were under the spell of his Diamond chant. During those days of long distance walking, each head of family used to carry a bamboo stick with two bundles balanced over his shoulders. Usually one bundle would contain rolled-up quilts, bedding, and clothes while the other bundle would contain cooking utensils, bowls, spoons, chopsticks, and pots and pans. Often, some bags of rice and salt tied up in strings would end up in the second bundle. It was ordinarily beneath my father's dignity to carry such a bamboo setup because he was a scholar, ranking higher than the peasant, the laborer, and the merchant according to the old Chinese tradition. But when Uncle Zhai carried two bundles, over his shoulder while my father had no more resources to hire a *tiaofu* for our family bundles it was time for my father to do his share.

Uncle Zhai said, "When I do my Diamond chant for you, you will walk as smooth as silk and as steady as a rock."

Although my mother and the rest of us were worried that my father would not last the better part of a day the way he swayed back and forth, taking ten steps in zigzags to cover Uncle Zhai's six steps, he lasted all day without taking more rest stops than most of the men on the road. Apparently Uncle Zhai's Diamond chant did the trick.

By sunset we finally arrived at the brick walls encircling an abandoned huge estate. Many refugee families had arrived ahead of us and had made it a crowded yard. In order not to walk all around to the front gate of the estate, people had made use of a broken section in the walls by walking over piles of broken bricks and stones to take the shortcut. Another man just ahead of us had slipped a little and nearly fell down over the fallen bricks. So my mother cautioned Father to be extra careful.

My father answered Mother, "That man was careless when he slipped. I will not slip."

Uncle Zhai immediately joined in, " I will do the Diamond chant for you. You can just go ahead and walk right through." Then he started mumbling again.

My father marched bravely through the opening in the wall with the two bundles balanced over his shoulder. When he was almost through the pile of bricks, we saw those bundles on his long stick beginning to shake back and forth. In the midst of the Diamond chant by Uncle Zhai, we heard a great thump as Father tripped on a loose piece of brick and fell over. We heard the breaking of china bowls and the clanging of metal against stones. Then there was silence.

We all ran quickly through the wall opening to see what had happened. Mother got there before everyone else. My father, red-faced, struggled to stand up with neither the stick nor the bundles on his shoulder. He was apparently unhurt as Mother tried to help him stand up. I bent and tried to pick up his spectacles for him as he patted his behind. I was glad those spectacles were not cracked as they slipped off his nose.

Uncle Zhai patted his own chest as he remarked, "Fortunately, I was reciting the Diamond chant for you. Otherwise, who knows, one of your legs might very well have been broken over those sharp bricks." My memory of that evening meal was eating rice out of three-fourths of a rice bowl while picking up vegetables with my chopsticks from two-thirds of a broken wok.

# Chapter 18.
## *I Danced for the Firewood*

With two halves of a broken wok, a few broken plates and some chipped and broken rice bowls being distributed in smaller bundles for all of us to carry, my father was happily relieved of his burden. From then on, he only had to carry the family quilt in a bundle on his back and there was no more need for balance. The bamboo stick became his walking stick. Once in a while he would pick up XiaoDi and let him sit on his shoulders as he had done before. Fortunately, XiaoDi was very skinny and was light in weight. But I also carried a small bundle.

This was a tortuous and slow trip over the long haul. But the toughest assignment for us children was to gather firewood. Finding fallen tree branches in the woods was hard enough in those days. For a fast running six-year-old, it still could be resolved. Oftentimes, however, just as I had found a nice piece and picked it up, it would be grabbed by some other bigger boy from another refugee family.

One day, I walked by a saw mill looking for some discarded pieces of remnants. But other bigger boys had already cleaned out the area. Then as I looked around the building, I found a small pile of split firewood neatly stacked in the rear entrance to the side. Without a second thought, I picked up three or four pieces and cradled them in my arms. A huge man appeared out of nowhere just as I was about to leave.

# Escape from Heng Yang:

He was very stern and intimidating as he said, "That is my firewood."

I was scared, but I tightly clutched the pieces of firewood and looked up at him, my legs shaking. After a moment of silence as he noticed my pitiful size he appeared softened a little and said, "If you sing a song and do a dance for me, I will let you have them."

Although I never did have much talent in singing or dancing, I slowly put down the firewood and started with the only song I knew:

> My baby brother is getting tired;
> His eyelids are getting heavier….. Heavier….
> My baby brother is getting very tired;
> He is getting sleepy……
> He will now fall into a good sleep…….

I kept my tears from falling as I sang this one song, while I twirled around in a dance mode. I remembered the previous time when I performed in front of my father's school faculty for a small silk flag and how I had lost it in the village fire set by Japanese soldiers. So in the middle of singing it the second time, my tears started to fall as I thought about my little silk flag and the happy times on my grandfather's farm. I really, really missed my silk flag! The man was apparently moved as he bent down and picked up those pieces of firewood and helped me cradle them in my arms again. I thanked him and slowly walked back to where my parents were waiting. This episode stayed in my memory so deeply that I later wrote a short story entitled " Dance" as I became an adult.

Finding firewood was something we children could do. But looking for food to feed everyone was an adult thing. Uncle Zhai and my father ran around trying to find anything they could for all of us to share. One day as we settled in a deserted temple in a village, it was getting dark. So with a torch in hand, Uncle Zhai and my father each went in a different direction. After some time Uncle Zhai came back with a long face and the extinguished torch in his hand. We knew he had failed to find a thing. But we kept a glimmer of

## *The Memoir of a Six-Year-Old Refugee Girl*

hope as Uncle Zhai started mumbling his Diamond chant for my father. Our stomachs growled along with his chanting as we waited.

Then all of a sudden, my father appeared in the doorway. With the biggest grin on his face, he unwrapped many layers of newspapers over a very large object. It was a huge pig's head! So Mother took it by the well and prepared it for a soup. I remember a nursery rhyme that went like this:

> Clapping hands, greasy bread,
> You sell lipsticks, I sell Ruche;
> Selling to Luzhou (we) lost our shirts!
> Buy a pig's head everybody shares;
> You can't chew the pig's head?
> Just roll it down the river bank;
> Ping, Pong…… Bang !

Mrs. Zhai supplied her large pot and helped Mother bring it to a boil and simmered it for a long time. Mother added some salt and some ginger and scallions. Later they handed us bowls of pork soup. It was the greatest soup I ever tasted in my whole life.

No one ever knew just how my father found that pig's head. But Uncle Zhai always gave credit to his chanting at the time. He was so devoted to his Diamond chant that one day when his ten-year-old daughter had a toothache with her cheek swollen like a big red apple, he started to chant for her. Uncle Zhai dipped his finger in water and drew a sign over her cheek. He chanted in a loud tone for quite some time. Then he asked her, " Don't you feel a lot better now?"

Although her swollen cheek grew even larger while trying not to cry, she saw the eagerness in her father's eyes and answered rather meekly, "Yes, I think I am feeling a little better."
So Uncle Zhai laughed heartily and said, "You see? As long as I recite the Diamond chant we can overcome almost any problem."

Our journey through GuiZhou became much easier to bear as

## Escape from Heng Yang:

we kept company with a humorous Uncle Zhai. Once in a while, we got to ride on a truck or a bus that burned charcoal. But GuiZhou Province was so full of mountains and treacherous hairpin turns that I once fell off the truck and suffered a huge cut on my nose. As I try to recall what had transpired, my survival from that fall could have been attributed to Uncle Zhai's Diamond chant. It was a miracle because I fell on a flat area around a bend of the road
when I lost my grip of the rope on top of the truck. If I had fallen one minute earlier or one minute later, I would have rolled down several hundred meters!

One evening we arrived at a small village and were warmly received by an old farmer and his wife. After supper we all sat around to chat with them. The farmer asked us where we were heading. So my father told him that we planned to hike over the next mountain ridge in hope to reach *Jianhe* county ( literally *Jianhe* means "sword river") the next day. He warned us that it was dangerous to go north at that time because a group of bandits had occupied the mountain area.

So Father said, "But we are just some poor refugees. What have we got to lose?"

The farmer said, "Some refugees sew their gold pieces in their garments or their quilts."

At that Uncle Zhai chimed in with his humor, "Yes, we might appear to be poor refugees, but we have lots of hidden treasure in our overcoats. Ho, Ho!"

The farmer said, "In that case you had better not cross this mountain."

Uncle Zhai, still laughing, answered, "Who's afraid of a few bandits? I would just recite the Diamond chant and they'd all disappear."

So we ventured onto that deserted mountain the next morning. It reminded me of the "Great Windy Mountain" which had divided Hunan from GuangXi provinces many weeks before. But then I was riding high in the saddle of Captain Tseng with his huge

## The Memoir of a Six-Year-Old Refugee Girl

arms protecting me the whole time. As we walked through tall grass and rocky areas, Uncle Zhai recited his famous Diamond chant. This went on for a couple of hours until we came to an area with a narrow path in front of us with high walls on both sides.

All of a sudden a man came out shouting at us and five or six men came from behind and formed a circle around us. Some of them had guns and some had big knives. Apparently they knew we were coming. Later my father said to my mother that he thought these bandits might have been informed by that old farmer. Those men took every bundle and package from us and forced us to remove our overcoats. They searched the pockets of my father and took his fountain pen along with a few sheets of paper money that were not worth much due to inflation at that time. Uncle Zhai continued to recite his chant as they emptied his pockets of whatever he carried.
Our two families shivered in the wind long after the bandits left us. Uncle Zhai claimed that if it weren't for his Diamond chant we'd all been killed.

As we moved on toward Jianhe county seat below us, Uncle Zhai mixed his chant with complaints about the lack of protection in Jianhe County and vowed to contact the local magistrate to voice his complaint. He even threatened to go to Guiyang and tell the governor of GuiZhou about this incident. He said, "If I get no satisfaction in GuiZhou, I'd go to the national court in ChongQing and sue this magistrate." None of us doubted his sincerity.

Soon it was dark and we all looked for fallen tree branches to make a fire. Uncle Zhai triumphantly produced some matches and a flattened match box from the inside of his cloth-sewn shoes and quickly started a fire. So we all huddled around the fire until day break. I fell asleep in my mother's lap as XiaoDi laid his head on my stomach.

My father held Qiling, my twin brother, while leaning on the side of a tree. But the morning chill woke us all up. Somehow the

## Escape from Heng Yang:

fire had burned out in the middle of the night. The next day, we hurried on down the mountain as the warm sun came out. By noon we arrived in the Jianhe county seat, which was quite a large town. Uncle Zhai kept his word by going straight to the office of the magistrate and reprimanded him for the lack of police protection.

The kind local magistrate was very tolerant as he repeatedly apologized to us and had his assistant find some old garments for us to keep warm and some food to feed us. He even located an old empty house to let us stay in town. Thus, Uncle Zhai finally calmed down and stopped his complaints. He soon thought of a new method for us to make some money, however. It was a short play, which he wrote to be acted on stage. The story of his stage play was based on our real-life experience. Even my parents, who were as conservative as they come, quickly agreed with this scheme, because it showed some promise. At least it would keep us all busy for a while.

# Chapter 19.
## *Yams Are Served!*

A stage with a curtain was set up at the corner of a main intersection in Jianhe town. I never did find out where that stage itself had come from. But during the war away from front lines, stage plays had become popular pastimes for everyone. The title of the play written by Uncle Zhai was,"Yams are served!"

So who would you guess were the main actors of the play? You've guessed it! They were my parents. But Ucle Zhai was the man behind the scene. In fact, he was the  writer, the producer, director, stage manager, costumes, sound effect, lighting and props man! Now when I think of it, I believe Ucle Zhai did have a lot of talent in doing stage plays. Under the circumstances our play came out quite up to par.

When our parents were busy rehearsing for the play, we were happy to do whatever we pleased without supervision. Later when they went on stage, we couldn't be more delighted, because my parents were made up and had to be dressed up for their parts. When all the town's people came to watch the show from below the stage, we were so proud of our parents as they became the center of attention.

Soon I became their most faithful audience as I hung onto every word they said in all their performances. I virtually memorized all their lines without even trying. My side job was to manage the curtain for them.

The story describes a small family with the husband (my father)

## Escape from Heng Yang:

getting ready to go to the front lines in order to fight the invading Japanese troops. He keeps saying goodbye to his young wife (my mother) who is trying to cook some yams for him before he leaves home. As they murmur to each other in sweet nothings, the bugle sounds from somewhere outside the little house (stage set) urging the husband to leave home and join his unit. The husband becomes quite nervous, but he keeps on talking about how he will miss her and the baby (the baby cries from backstage). So the young wife goes backstage to calm the baby down as the husband strolls back and forth on stage in front of the window and looks out. When the baby goes back to sleep, the wife comes back out to say goodbye once more. Then the bugle sounds again.

Wife "Let me go in and check on the yams." She leaves.
Husband strolls.

She soon comes out to say that the yams are not yet ready. The bugle sounds; the baby cries; the young wife goes in and out and the husband keeps on strolling in front of the window. Then when the wife goes back once more to check on the yams, her husband jumps out of the window and disappears (gone to the front lines).

Then the wife comes on stage with a plate full of steaming yams and yells, "Yams are served! Yams are served!" She sees an empty room with her husband gone (horse hoofs galloping away farther and farther). She runs to the window as she drops the plate on the floor. The plate breaks while the yams come tumbling down. Amidst the bugle sounds, the baby crying, the horse hoofs galloping and the young wife weeping, I would draw the curtain to a close.

Thus, this short stage play not only describes the deep loving feelings between the two young people but also portrays the atmosphere among the patriotic Chinese during the war of defense against a belligerent and barbaric invading Japanese army deep in China. It was a tiny story distilled out of the sentiment from every person forced to leave his or her home after witnessing atrocity after atrocity that was systematically displayed by the invading forces. It was the worst of times. So this stage play was Uncle Zhai's success.

## *The Memoir of a Six-Year-Old Refugee Girl*

The audience was extremely moved by each performance as they clapped and hollered "Hao! Hao (good)!" But soon they all dispersed leaving very little money for the show. So after a few days of enthusiastic stage plays, coupled with broken plates and spilled yams, our management team quickly ran short of funds, it was "curtains" for good.

The kind-hearted magistrate of Jianhe County was apologetic as he was unable to find the bandits who had robbed us and saw how hard we tried to survive through stage plays. He arranged two county jobs for Uncle Zhai and my father and sincerely invited us to stay. We had become so tired of the long journey at this point that my parents decided to stay in Jianhe for a while. The temporary arrangement lasted more than six months in the end.

# Chapter 20.
## *We Won! We Won! The War Is Over!*

Those one hundred fifty some days in Jianhe were probably the most peaceful and uneventful ordinary days for us as refugees. Mother learned to make shoes so that we all had new shoes to wear for a change. My father kept busy teaching and doing odd jobs. We attended a local elementary school and made some friends.

One day, Father came home with the large horn of a water buffalo. It turned out he had met a chops-and-seal-carving master and had started to take lessons from this man. Then my father found the trunk section of a huge bamboo tree. He carved it into a very nice desktop container for brushes and fountain pens. Then he wrote and carved two characters on the side of the brush container: "*JingJie*" meaning "unbending resolve in a righteous decision." But after he finished carving those two characters, he became very quiet and unhappy with himself. He actually became depressed. Even Uncle Zhai's humor could not make him smile anymore.

Once again we started on our way for ChongQing. This time, Uncle Zhai decided to stay in Jianhe County, so we were on our own. This time we could afford mule carts and donkeys and went much faster. Funny thing was, when we finally arrived in the vicinity of ChongQing, we came across a group of people in a village running and shouting the exciting news of the announcement of surrender by the emperor of Japan over the radio.

So we joined the mob by yelling, "We won! We won! The War is over!

# Escape from Heng Yang
(not to scale)

This drawing shows the route of escape by the Chen family.

They went South West from Heng Yang toward GuangXi, met up with Captain Tseng just before the Hunan border, crossed a mountain into GuangXi, through Dong An (not shown), Guilin where they found her two brothers and bid goodbye to Captain Tseng.

They proceeded to Rong'an, got sick, were rescued and got into a small boat upstream to Rong Jiang, walked to JianHe, stayed for several months, then North West to ChongQing in the summer of 1945.

*Escape from Heng Yang: The Memoir of a Six-Year-Old Refugee Girl* is a reminiscence that provides the reader with insight into the Japanese invasion and occupation of China during WWII. It is the autobiographical story of Chung Yao who, with her two brothers and their parents, faced much adversity as they traveled from their home in Heng Yang to the distant Chongqing. Ironically, when they reach Chongqing after a long and perilous journey, the enemy is conceding defeat and China has won the war.

In Chinese tradition, Chung Yao's professor father was socially ranked higher than merchants, laborers, or peasants because he was a scholar. That this family, unused to privation and manual labor, with three small children, could survive the arduous and hazardous journey described is a testament to the human spirit. The children walked, rode in baskets, rode on horseback, and rode on extremely crowded trains while their parents had to sell all of their possessions and earn money at unfamiliar activities from cooking yams to sell to acting in a play about yam selling, and ultimately the family had to depend on the kindness of strangers. Through all of these adventures, the reader learns of one Chinese family's point of view of WWII rarely seen in the English language.

## *About the Author*

Eugene Lo Wei was born in LeShan, China, during the war against Japanese invasion. His parents had to escape from Nanjing just prior to the Rape of Nanjing holocaust in 1937, three years before Eugene was born. Eugene came to Chicago, Illinois, with his parents when he was eighteen, freshly graduated from high school.

He later graduated from the University of Illinois with honors in chemistry and again from MIT with a master's degree. After four more years at the University of Colorado in Boulder, Eugene taught college chemistry for six years before working in the water treatment industry. He joined the Alliance for Preserving the Truth of Sino-Japanese War (APTSJW) in 1993.

In 2002 he founded the American Museum of Asian Holocaust WWII in Falls Creek, Pennsylvania. He is currently married to Amy Dongmei Hu from China.